Information management
and
archival data

90 0138767 X

Th

Information management and archival data

Michael Cook

LIBRARY ASSOCIATION PUBLISHING
LONDON

Published by
Library Association Publishing Ltd
7 Ridgmount Street
London WC1E 7AE

First published 1993

British Library Cataloguing in Publication Data

Cook, Michael
  Information Management and Archival Data
  I. Title
  025

  ISBN 1-85604-053-4

Typeset in 10/12 pt Garamond from author's disks by Saxon Graphics Ltd, Derby.

Printed and made in Great Britain by Bookcraft (Bath) Ltd.

Contents

Preface

This book started ·with a phone call from Library Association Publishing. Would it be a good idea, they wondered, to prepare a new edition of Sir Hilary Jenkinson's *Manual of archive administration*? I put this question to the current generation of student archivists who were following Liverpool University's course for the Master of Archive Administration degree. Their response was quite unequivocal: it was 'No'.

No lack of respect was intended to Jenkinson, the great master of archival practice in Britain. His book, published in 1922, provided the necessary impulse for the foundation of the archival profession in this country. It was a perceptive and liberal manual, and served the first generations well. It proved a good foundation for later developments, even though some of these would have seemed quite unlikely at the time it was originally written. But it cannot be denied that it was written from a narrow and specialized standpoint, one which has since come to look increasingly remote from daily reality. Older archivists, myself included, can still not bring themselves to jettison its standards and principles entirely, or even its language, but we can see clearly enough that the manual can no longer serve as a textbook for a first-entry training course. In fact, no single book can do this any more. We need to work at producing a body of literature which can support training courses, set and disseminate standards, and lay a foundation for further development.

Even by 1977, when my *Archives administration* was published, it was clear that 'it is no longer possible for one person to write a complete survey of professional practice in the administration of archives. Too many specialities have developed .... Among the important subjects which are not dealt with in detail here are ... technical developments and standards in description (cataloguing).' It was with a slight shock of surprise that I reread these words while preparing the text of this book for publication. It is sometimes difficult to believe in the possibility that the thoughts of today originated in the past. Fifteen years ago did we really see the road ahead so clearly? It has been a stony road, but after all it did lead fairly straight.

This, then, is the promised book on technical developments and standards in description. An effort has been made to minimize the specialist character that this objective suggests. The approach taken has been to explain and discuss the principles and techniques of professional practice as they seem to stand at present, as they have been affected by the new description standards. A fairly wide view has been taken. Records management, for example, has received some attention. This was because standards of information service within it have also been profoundly influenced by advances in archival description (would this have been foreseen in 1977?); and moreover it is a subject that has recently been developing rapidly into new forms.

The description standards on which this book is based are the second edition of the *Manual of archival description* (MAD2), and the *General international standard archival description* (ISAD(G)) produced in 1992 by the International Council on Archives. Other description standards exist, and no doubt by the time this book has appeared more will have developed. So it goes.

In writing a new book on archival management, I also had a more general aim. This was to update and restructure the literature available for training. I always have one type of reader in mind - the enthusiastic and able students and beginners who have suffered my teaching for a quarter of a century, in Britain and in Africa. There have been so many changes, it was unreasonable to lose this opportunity of setting out the consequences of some of them. I am grateful to the student body and wish them well; they have been an appreciative audience, and I have learnt most of what I know from them.

One other matter should be explained here. This book assumes that archival description as a practice, and the management of archives more generally, is a subject of some interest for society at large. It is not a specialism which lurks in its own corner and has no effects on the world outside. Archives are all around us. They are a major and irreplaceable source of information. Every organization, public or private, government or commercial, lives on its internal information resources. A high proportion of all administrative expenditure goes on creating, storing, using and disposing of records. Every information service has an archival aspect. The proper management of these resources is of direct interest to the conduct of modern societies.

In some ways this fact has been tacitly admitted by British society, as it has been by others. Throughout the second half of the 20th century, archivists have belonged to a professional group which has consistently developed and grown in numbers and expertise. The Society of Archivists has grown from a membership of only a few score in the 1950s to about 1,300 in 1992, and this growth has continued, on a small scale but without perceptible interruption, through all the recessions of recent decades. This professional group has been remarkably active in developing professional standards, and has achieved this by self-help and by the personal commitment of its members. Where the British system has failed has been in developing a framework of law and standards in the public sector. I fear that this failure mars our work now and will be very severely regretted in the future. It is particularly sad to comment on it at this moment, when the foundation work of Jenkinson is being both undermined and celebrated.

It is pleasant to record thanks to the many colleagues and friends who have helped, and whose help was indeed indispensable. Special thanks are recorded to the two collaborators in the work of developing a description standard: Kristina Grant and Margaret Procter. I am grateful to my immediate colleagues in the Archives Unit of Liverpool University – Adrian Allan, Andrea Owens and Lyn Naylor – for their forbearance and support.

Help has also been received from several institutions, and thanks are offered to them with acknowledgement. The Society of Archivists and the Research and Development Department of the British Library both gave grants towards the initial research; funds for some of the meetings which were necessary have come from Unesco, the International Council on Archives, and the British Council.

The following archives services and individual colleagues have kindly allowed their work to be quoted or used: Charles Dollar, Frank Evans and others at the National Archives and Records Administration of the USA; Ian Dunn, Jonathan Pepler, and Caroline Williams and the Cheshire Record Office; Adam Green and the Somerset Record Office; Nicholas Kingsley and the Gloucestershire Record Office; Christopher Kitching and the Royal Commission on Historical Manuscripts; James McGrath and the Strathclyde University Archives; Harold Naugler and Sue Gavrel, and the National Archives of Canada; Carl Newton; Margaret Procter and the Merseyside Record Office; David Robinson and the Surrey Record Office; Michael Roper and several other members of the staff of the Public Record Office; Richard Storey and Alistair Tough and the Modern Record Centre of

Warwick University; Keith Sweetmore and the West Yorkshire Archives Service; Marcia Taylor and Bridget Winstanly and the ESRC Data Archive (University of Essex); Christopher Williams and the Clwyd Record Office; Gareth Williams and the Gwynedd Archives Service. Thanks and grateful acknowledgement are due to the National Archives and Records Administration of the USA; Crown Copyright material held in the Public Record Office is produced by permission of the Controller of Her Majesty's Stationery Office.

Michael Cook
Archival Description Project
University of Liverpool

Abbreviations

AACR2	*Anglo-American cataloguing rules*, 2nd edn
APPM2	*Archives, personal papers and manuscripts*, 2nd edn
DRO	Departmental Records Officer
ICA	International Council on Archives
ISAD(G)	*General international standard archival description*
MAD2	*Manual of archival description*, 2nd edn
PRO	Public Record Office (London)
RAD	Rules for Archival Description
RM	Records management
SCONUL	Standing Conference of National and University Libraries

1

The management of information, archives and records

Every organization collects, generates and manages information. It is an aspect of life which is inescapable; it is true of all organizations, whatever their purpose or character. The staffing structures and activities which are associated with information management are actually – but not always explicitly – built by powerful societal forces into every work activity. In the offices of every kind of organization, whether in the public or in the private sector, most of the day for most of the people is spent in handling information. A great deal of the cost of administration goes in providing the conditions needed for them to do it. It is possible to do it well, and to do it badly; rationally or by thoughtlessly following custom. It is possible to capture and keep the right or the wrong information for the support of any activity; it is possible to lose information and also to find it.

The management of information takes many forms. It is not always obvious that a particular activity is actually an aspect of information management. Since the handling of information has always taken place, in every age, many of the work processes involved are called something else. The term 'information management' is a recent one, but gathering data, telling people about decisions taken, issuing instructions, recording precedents, are activities which are ages old. Some organizations today have tried to draw information-handling processes together and put them under the control of an information manager. In fact, so widespread are information operations that information managers are rarely able to do more than coordinate some of the most prominent of them. Other organizations continue the older way, in which information operations continue in a dispersed and uncoordinated manner. The difference between these two approaches is the difference between central planning and control, and dispersed and decentralized methods.

In fact, the experience of Eastern Europe shows us that it is never possible or desirable to control everything from the centre, and we can see that dispersed and decentralized activities are not always chaotic. This book is about aspects of information management, but it does not set out to argue that highly centralized methods of management are the best or only way. In real life, people are constantly confronted by problems of information control, and they are practised at producing solutions to them. In every office, indeed in every home, individuals solve information problems daily. Coordinating their activities may be useful, may often be necessary. It will never be possible to coordinate everything.

Information activities can be analysed into groups, which can be given different names to describe the various facets of the work. These groups of activities indeed reflect the nature of many human concerns, which have to be generated, put through a process, and then used or dispersed. Each of the groups contains a range of different operations, and is multi-faceted.

The present is a fleeting moment, each second passing into history in the blink of an eye. Information is often thought of as something current, up to date, evanescent. Some kinds of information are like this, but many other kinds have much more static, permanent or long-lasting qualities. Every information-related activity has a retrospective aspect, and most items of information have two uses: one as related to the present, one as related to conditions which previously existed, in the past a moment ago. This is true for the materials of all forms of information service. Research scientists need the most current data; politicians or decision-makers need the latest report, the most recent statistical aggregation; letter-writers need a current address.

This means that the information that passes out of currency should be distinguished from information still current. It must be removed from the current file, put through an appraisal process, and put in another file, or disposed of. These activities – retiring data from current, appraising it, putting it somewhere else, and using it in a different way – are the central concerns of this book; they are the processes used in records management and by an archives service. It must also be recognized that every information service, however pledged to up-to-dateness, actually has to carry out similar processes. Every information service has a retrospective function, an archival potential.

In the same way, an archives service also has an up-to-date aspect,

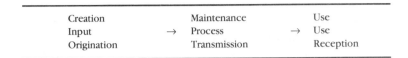

Creation		Maintenance		Use
Input	→	Process	→	Use
Origination		Transmission		Reception

Figure 1.1 Sequence of activities in information work

a way in which it can be said to be handling current information. This aspect is prominent when one is referring to the archives as part of the information services of an active institution, or when it is considered as an institution in itself. Archivists have to consider how it is that the information relevant to them is generated, processed and used, and some of the work they do is part of these activities. An archives service too can best be analysed by using a version of the threefold analysis shown in Figure 1.1. If every information service has a retrospective – an archival – aspect, so then every archives service has a significance for current operations. The recognition of this fact, so often obscured in the past, is one of the main reasons for writing this book. The management of archives (and records) is an inescapable part of information management.

The nature of the business

Information management is a term which describes a set of activities, or theoretical fields of activity. The activities are mostly not recently invented, but the use of the term is characteristic of the preoccupations dominant in the last decades of the 20th century. The recognition that information (although a complex and elusive commodity) is something of value to most people and most organizations, and which needs to be managed, is one which has come slowly and incompletely. It was slow in part because of the nature of the information services which existed before the 'information age' began: libraries, documentation services, records management programmes, and archives. The basic aims of these services, and their physical forms, were not in their original shape conducive to building them into programmes which could be seen as a whole, or as agencies for handling what were different forms of the same commodity. There are still tendencies which separate the different services and keep them distinct from each other.

In what follows, the discussion centres upon two of these services:

3

records management and archives management. In concentrating upon these, similarities and overlap with the other types of information service will not be overlooked.

It is important to be clear what is meant by the terms. The central theme of this book is the operation of an *archives service*; part of an archives service is a *records management* operation. Records management programmes also exist (in fact certainly much more often) as services quite distinct from archives. The difference between archives and records – the materials which define these two services – has therefore to be marked as strongly as possible. It is a distinction which is well founded in the (English-language) professional literature of the last three decades, but which has been confused, and continues to be confused in daily usage, by a peculiarity of British history.

The origins of organized archival practice in Britain lie far back in the period when organized and continuous administration was first coming into being. It was associated with records management – the measures taken to create, store and retrieve the record of government and the courts – even at that early period. Government has always shown a generally greater consciousness of the need for archival service than any other type of administration. This is because it is important that public decisions and awards should be made permanent and binding, and that consistent policies should be followed; and because of the personal vanity of rulers.

In the beginning, the recording agencies within British governments were mainly attached to the legal system, and law courts acquired the important function of acting as the principal keepers of records. The concept of courts of record emerged, and over the passage of centuries this was the traditional base upon which government built its archives service. In 1838, as one of many administrative reforms undertaken at the period, the first Public Records Act established the Public Record Office on the site of one of the principal legal recording centres, the Rolls Chapel in London's Chancery Lane.[1] The PRO was from the first intended to house the archives of government, but the use of the term 'record' followed directly from the usage of the courts, as well as being then the word in common use. Nearly a century later, local government in its turn began to set up archival repositories, and simply followed the tradition in naming the new establishments as 'county record offices'. Though today the usage is sometimes challenged, it is still established. The consequence is that the term 'record' is often used interchangeably, in Britain, with the term 'archive'.

Despite this confusion of terms, the English language permits a clear definition for each, which has been confirmed in most of the literature on the subject since the 1950s. The distinction has even been taken into French and Spanish professional usage, even though these languages do not have ready-made words for the two terms.[2] *Records* are information media which are created in the course of business by an organization, and kept because they are of use in that business. *Archives* are a subset of the records: they are the records which have passed an appraisal test, have been selected because of their possible value in other kinds of reference, and have been placed in an archival repository, or at least allocated to a permanent retention category.

It is important to note that neither records nor archives are defined with respect to the recording medium. Most examples of both are on paper, doubtless, but the medium can be anything – recorded sound or vision, machine-readable disks, microforms, parchment or papyrus. The message may be encoded in any way: graphics and cartographic materials are equally included, as are pictorial messages, whether drawn, painted or photographic.

It is also important to note that neither definition mentions date as a significant feature. The date of materials is indeed used as a management criterion in appraisal and as a way of controlling access to them, but in principle either records or archives can be of any date, nor is it necessary, in principle again, that documents should be out of currency in order to be considered as archives.

The material which is the subject of archives management has been selected in order to promote the exploitation of values other than those important for current reference. Archives are usually consulted for their retrospective value, because they inform about previous situations, or about the way situations came to be, rather than because they give currently valid information. Retrospective values can of course be very important in current investigations, as well as in the examination of what happened in the remote past. Archives are just as valuable to students of modern society as they are to medieval historians. In fact, some understanding of what archives are and how they may be interpreted is actually necessary to every citizen, even though only a few may become regular users of an archive repository.

Records management shares with archives an interest in retrospective values. It also shares with information science an interest in current information. Since its basic material, records, are mainly valuable because of their retrospective character, the point at which RM is most concerned with current values is the point where currency lasts longest – where legal precedent or unchanging information is involved, or where the recorded information maintains its relevance longest for current concerns.

The classic British writer on archive administration, Sir Hilary Jenkinson,[3] defined archives by stressing their official relationships: 'Archives are documents which formed part of an official transaction and were preserved for official reference'.[4] The official nature of the archives confirmed, he thought, their impartiality as evidence, for they were not intended as other than administrative tools created by administrators for their own convenience, and were preserved only by them and only for that convenience. A consequence of this definition, for Jenkinson, was that an unbroken history of custody by the creating organization or its delegates was necessary to preserve, or to demonstrate, this quality of impartiality: 'We do not wish to press for a purely legal definition of custody; but ... Archive quality is dependent upon the possibility of proving an unblemished line of responsible custodians.'[5]

In later years, Jenkinson's doctrine of continuous custody came to be exaggerated, almost to the point of absurdity. For, as he himself pointed out,[6] historical documents which had no archival status, or which had strayed from archival custody at some period, could be considered as evidence just as much as those which had always been in the archives. An examination of what their custodial history had actually been, was simply part of the process of authenticating them. Because there has been some misunderstanding of the principle of continuous archival custody, an attempt at redefinition would be useful.

Both archives and records services operate by delegation. It is the natural business of any organization to manage its records and archives, simply because these are both functions of an organized body. This can be demonstrated quite simply. When there is an inquiry which calls for records to be consulted, the director of the organisation is asked for them. When the American space observatory programme failed in June 1990, because the telescope mirror was incorrectly designed, one of the first actions of the government investigators was to impound records of the space agency. This action

6

was not only to ensure that the records would not be destroyed or falsified, but also simply to allow the inquiry team to find the information they needed. In the same way, researchers wishing to study a subject approach the modern representatives of organizations connected with the topic. They expect, or hope, that these representatives have kept first the records, and then the archive.

It is possible for organizations to delegate some of their records management functions and all of their archival functions to external agencies. Records storage and retrieval, for example, can be delegated to a storage firm. Archives can be deposited with a public-service or academic repository.

Wherever archives have been deposited with a repository, the custody of those archives has been delegated by the originators (or their representatives) to the repository. This must always be true. Sometimes the act of delegation has been obscurely buried in the past, or must be inferred. Where archival materials have been rescued from destruction in the ruins of an abandoned plant, it is hard to give credit for intelligent delegation to the organization which created them, and which abandoned them there. It is still reasonable to assume that there has been delegation, for if ownership can be proved (and generally, a study of the provenance of the materials will also give indications of the ownership), then delegation must have occurred. There are precedents for the view that the archives of an organization are part of its assets. They can be given a monetary value, and if the organization goes into liquidation, the receiver may order that they should be valued for sale.[7] Delegation is an essential feature of archives service, and helps to define the materials which are held and managed.

If we can recognize that there is a principle of delegation then we can also see that it is one of the basic duties and functions of organizations to manage their own records and archives. Delegation is a device which can be used in certain circumstances, but it should not be regarded as necessary or universally desirable.

An archives service which belongs to and continuously serves the organization which creates the records, must logically be regarded as the norm from which others take their model. This is the case with central government (or national) archives services, such as the PRO. Where archives services make an unconsidered general practice of accepting archival materials on deposit from unconnected organizations, some questions might be asked about the professional ethics involved. On the one hand, the archives service is providing technical and specialist services which the originating organization may be unable to provide for itself. These services include aspects which the originating organization might itself be unwilling to set up at all, such as open access by members of the public. They also include, of course, conservation and management to good standards.

On the other hand, if the act of delegation is not fully considered, it may result in very defective archives services which do not relate well to RM procedures in the originator. Where a manufacturing firm, for example, has deposited its basic core of older archives with the local county archives service, it is possible (perhaps likely) that it may neglect the management processes, appraisal and disposal of records, which keep the archive up to date. Having got rid of the problem of a backlog archive accumulation, they may neglect the problems that led to it being there. There is no doubt that in the past archives services have often been too ready to accept the backlog accumu-lation of obsolete records, probably stored in the cellar or in an outhouse, as if it were the whole archive. Collecting in the backlog may thus have been thought the primary and/or even the whole duty of a local or specialist repository.

Sometimes the delegation of archival duties is difficult to perceive. Visitors to the British Library's India Office Records, for example, need not necessarily know that in former periods the predecessors of this office managed the archives of the India Office and indirectly of its forerunner the East India Company. For many, it is sufficient to see it as a specialist branch of the British Library and a research centre of distinction, which happens to specialize in Indian sources. In this case, the organization which created the records has passed away, and so there can be no further relationship with it. A modern county council, however, may delegate its archival duties to its county record office, and continues to create new records daily. The record office may or may not provide records management services (the tradition is mixed here), but normally exercises the delegated archival powers. Nevertheless, the repository appears to its users as a distinct organization, and may function consciously as a centre of research and reference in its own right.

The principle of delegation should be called in aid, to support the idea that the relationship between a delegated repository and the creating organization is a continuing one. What has been delegated is more the function (of managing the archives) than just the materials. Thus delegation is more than the question of custody, and Jenkinson's original statement of the principle of continuous custody may be seen as rather too narrow.

There is a second principle which can be called upon to supplement this part of the definition. Archives and records are information media which are generated from within the system, whereas books, other publications and technical documentation are brought in from outside it.[8] This aspect of the definition is the reverse side of the principle of delegation.

Records and archives management are defined by the material they deal with, which is their stock in trade. Because of this, the two disciplines have a constructive procedure: they use evidence produced from surviving material to provide intellectual explanations for what is or has been. Because certain records or archives exist, we know or can deduce certain facts. This means that the subjects of study which use records or archives as primary sources tend themselves to be defined by the categories represented by the materials.

Researchers who come to an archives office to pursue a subject enquiry often find there is a mismatch between their subject categories (which are drawn from the outside world) and the categories of information represented in the finding aids (which are drawn from the materials). The same mismatch exists to some extent in all information services, but it is very marked in records and archives work. The broader field of information management is not confined to any particular material as such. Its essential commodity may often reside in records or documents, but the discipline takes its starting-point from the requirements of the user. By defining what the user's information needs are, an attempt can be made to supply them. This is a reversal of the aims of records and archives management service, as traditionally stated. Records and archives therefore, while clearly belonging to the general field of information management, have strongly marked characteristics which distinguish them from other disciplines in the field, and which have important effects on the design of finding aids.

There have always been two fairly distinct types of archives service. The kind most obvious to external users and the public are those which are public institutions in their own right. They might manage the archives (and perhaps even the records) of a particular organization and its satellites, but once the materials have been transferred to the repository, the user services based upon them take on the appearance and attitudes of a single-purpose institution.

The other kind of repository might be called 'internal', and has a programme which chiefly operates within the parent organization. Even so it may have much of the character of a specialized research facility. Those researching questions relating to the development of the steel industry in the north-west of England should approach the British Steel Records Centre at Shotton.[9] The Centre's main concern is the management of records in the company, but it contains archival materials and provides facilities for research access. There are many other examples, chiefly in the private sector, of repositories which have user services but whose chief work lies within the controlling organization.

The character of neither of these models is affected, still less defined, by the repository's policy on the acquisition and deposit of external materials. In the British tradition, it is quite normal for record offices to seek and receive the archives of outside bodies on deposit. It is quite difficult to find an example of an archives service of any kind that has not done so. Manuscript libraries or departments look on external acquisitions as their only source of new material. At the other extreme, outside deposits would be rare in a repository which was accustomed to concentrate on records management. Most institutions between these extremes would have a collection policy more or less active.

The principles and standards which are the subject of this book should apply to all kinds of archives service. There cannot be a single, unalterable model. The nature of the service offered must vary according to the nature of the employing body, the nature of its business and the records it creates, the kind and level of staffing, the suitability of the accommodation occupied, the budget, and other factors. Possibly the most important factor is the repository staff's own perception of their aims, backed by specific statements of the service's mission. The statement of aims is therefore of great importance.

Information transmission theory

The best-known theoretical model for the transmission of information from a source to a receiver was originally devised to explain how telephonic communication works. In the context of librarianship,

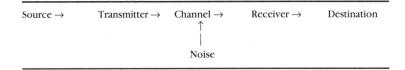

Figure 1.2 The communication process within an information service

analogies like the Shannon-Weaver model were used to explain this process graphically, and to introduce concepts and the labels applied to them. We should accept the principle that information is first held in a source, and then reaches the understanding of a receiver (a user) by going through a series of processes: encoding, passage through a channel, decoding. In Figure 1.2 readers will recognize a reflection of the grouped functions of information work shown in Figure. 1.1. The model also illustrates how at each of these intermediate stages the communication process may be interfered with by 'noise', irrelevant and obstructive signals. In addition, very few messages are totally self-sufficient, so that some common information passes from source to user through other channels: archives work illustrates this well.

The claim has been made that records and archives management operate, like other information services, under the terms of models like this, without introducing any new feature.[10] The proposition has not been formally questioned; but it is also true that there is a perception that this kind of theoretical analysis is irrelevant to real professional concerns and without much practical effect. In fact, it is important that records managers and archivists do understand that their work falls within the discipline of information science, and therefore can be analysed in accordance with theoretical explanations of it.

The importance of this perception is twofold. From it comes an openness to professional orientations which ought to allow or promote apt responses to new developments and technologies. These orientations suggest appropriate structures and relationships between structures, which are important when designing an archives or records service. They also provide a technical vocabulary which is illuminating and promotes coherence within the broader profession.

There is a more fundamental consequence, which was also referred to at the end of the discussion on definitions. Accepting the principle of user primacy can alter the priorities and objectives of archival practice. Instead of building a programme solely aimed at the

11

control, use and disposition of materials which happen to be there, archivists and records managers may come to start their work with an analysis of the universe of information produced by the organization, and its relationship to the larger universe of information brought in from outside and used by it. This starting-point at once brings them into a direct relationship with the other information services likely to be encountered within a complex organization.

Professional processes

An important contribution of information science is that there is a distinction between the carrier and the content – the medium and the message – in the management of documents. This is a distinction which has not always been recognized in records or archives management, although it has great importance in several areas of central direction and planning, as well as in designing finding aids. Most procedures in RM and in archives management are concerned with the physical control of actual documents – not always on a paper medium, but most often. The two disciplines have in the past been entirely described in terms of document control, which means that training has concentrated on processes, of recording, transmission, retrieval, use, storage and disposal. The following table lists some of the processes which have been included.

Recording
   Rules for writing down the content of messages, e.g. telephone notes, memoranda
   Methods of composing, transmitting and filing of correspondence
   Distribution and filing of internal directives
   Commissioning of statistical and other reports
   Data capture, use of forms
   Committee structure and servicing
   Fieldwork
   Surveying a defined subject or functional field
   Certain legal procedures
Transmission
   Registry and filing systems
   Movement and storage of mail
   Email
   Conferencing

Information retrieval
  Records centre operations
  Selective dissemination of information (SDI)
  Statistical and research services
  Micrographics
  Xerography
  Publishing
Use
  External research access
  Educational services
  Genealogical, family history and personal research
  Local studies
Storage and disposal
  Appraisal
  Retention policy
  General records security
  Waste disposal and recycling
  Conservation and repair
  Storage control
  Equipment and monitoring
  Disaster plan
  Vital records plan

All the activities in this list, together with others, can be considered relevant to some aspects of records or archives management. Not all are exercised by any one particular archives service, but then in real life many archives services actually undertake more, and all can be illustrated by the work of at least one archives or records service working at the present day in Britain.

Structures within record-creating organizations

The place of a records or archives service within the organization depends on the place allocated to information services generally. It is important to the success of the service that the administrative and financial structures should be well designed.

Figure 1.3 has been developed from observation of practice and especially of recent changes since the publication of Carl Newton's study in 1981.[11] It assumes that there is an overall position for an information manager, who will probably have other responsibilities also. The figure shows three main sectors:

- communications and computing
- library and documentation
- records and archives.

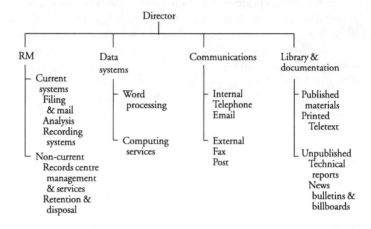

Figure 1.3 Information structures within an organization

However the information services may be structured, it is impossible to avoid a close connection between the archives and records services and communications and computing. This statement would have been absurd a few years ago. At that time computing, in organizations of any size, was usually concentrated in a single large machine, environmentally protected, whose tasks would be concentrated on finance and staffing. Although some archives and records management operations were remarkably successful at using the resources of this type of computing service, even as far back as the late 1970s, it would have been foolish to think that there could be a close, let alone a necessary, connection between records or archives and computers. This was especially so because information work seemed to be going in the direction of data processing. DP departments were totally alien in technique and objective from both records management and archives administration.

The situation is now quite different. Large central computers are disappearing, and are being replaced by networks of personal computers or workstations, and in any case senior and middle management are by now quite accustomed to having their own PCs or terminals, and using them for many office tasks. Communications by electronic channels are now common and rapidly becoming more so, even though their development has been less rapid and less uniform than was once predicted. The information manager has a vital interest in the development of communications systems via the computer terminals, and must at all costs be close to the technical side of this. One of the necessary measures is the maintenance of discipline over separate departments and outlying branches, so as to ensure that they do not start developing separate systems using incompatible software or hardware. This aspect of institutional development is central to the successful progress of the organization itself, and must bring information development close to senior management in its planning function.

What has tended to replace automatic data processing as a distinct set of technical operations is the work of statisticians or statistical intelligence units. Using techniques from the behavioural and social sciences these relate directly to decision-makers in the organization. They also customarily have a programme for the collection of data useful for their statistical work. These data come partly from within, operating data from departments, etc., and partly from without, showing the economic or environmental conditions. This is clearly an information service which has great vitality, and a close relationship to senior management. There ought also to be a link with the other information services, some of which will acquire and hold relevant data.

Figure 1.3, which really describes the situation within a large organization, shows records and archives in the same sector, and suggests that archives should be subordinate to records services. This situation is not uncommon, particularly where there has been American influence. It is not necessarily advocated here (nor do we advocate the alternative, where RM is subordinate to archives management). The diagram merely shows that in the context of information management there appears to be a closer connection between RM and archives than between either of these and the other two sectors.

There are other ways of looking at this connection, and to show this, Figure 1.4 reproduces an earlier model, which is concentrated

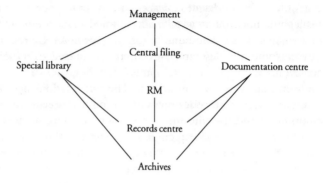

Figure 1.4 Internal information services

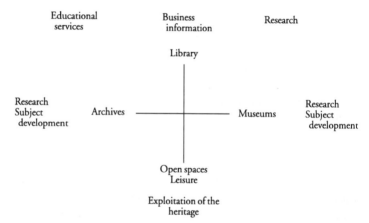

Figure 1.5 External information services

on the relationship of the three specialized information programmes within an organization. If Figures 3 and 4 are compared, it will be seen how much the information management field has opened up in recent years.

Figure 1.4 shows the information services which might operate within a large organization. This would include a local government authority or a government department, although the most typical examples are to be found in large national or multi-national firms in the private sector. A different model, illustrated in Figure 1.5, should be chosen if we look at the role and structure of information services oriented to the general public. Here too there is an evident tendency to link the archives services to other types of public service, but there is still some uncertainty as to the best way to link them, and which services to choose. The range of choice is limited by the range of activities which by law and custom are permitted to local government in Britain.

It seems likely that we should examine the relationships between archives services and other services within the parent organization or outside it, because there are hints that they do not have sufficient inherent resources and capabilities to exist as free-standing institutions. In the private sector it is quite natural (though not universal) to regard archives as a specialist aspect of records management. In the public sector, although it has been normal to treat 'record offices' as independent services, it is increasingly common to see them merged into larger groupings.

The services most often chosen to link with the archives service are as follows:

    public libraries generally
    local history and research/reference libraries
    business intelligence services
    museums
    education support services
    heritage and tourist centres
    leisure and community services
    legal services.

Because of the relative sizes of the units involved, it generally appears that the archives service becomes a junior partner in the amalgamation. For this reason it is very important that the right mixture should be chosen. From the user's point of view the creation of joint services of this kind offers great potential. Areas of study or groups of activities which have been kept arbitrarily separate for generations, because of institutional boundaries, are now being brought together. For the first time, planners are able to look straight at user needs, and at the overall pattern of information provision, and plan for services to meet those needs. From the point of view of successful managers, the development is good because it provides them with a better career structure. It is good for intermediate and paraprofessional staff for the same reason. All that is lost is the old institutional loyalty, which, although not entirely bad, certainly had a narrowing effect on the outlook of archives staff.

17

Information need

If there is truly to be a shift of emphasis from the care of the materials to the provision of service to the user, then we must learn what users wish to know. Some answers to this question are available from the experience of archivists who have been providing public service for many decades. These are only partial answers, for they are based on the observation of users who actually attend to consult documents they know to be there. The great bulk of these are in pursuit of family history. To give a complete answer would demand some further research, for there are a number of unknown variables. Some of these are listed below:

1 The nature of the core collections of archives services, and the nature of the finding aids provided. The older holdings of archives services are often under-used because to use them it is necessary to have a degree of prior information which is obtained only by an élite. Historically, these materials were among the earliest to be professionally managed, and the finding aids sometimes appear the least practised.

2 A lack of infrastructural knowledge and technique in the user public (although this is gradually being overcome).

3 There has been a consensus that the prime task of archivists should be the acquisition of new materials, and the next task in priority was the proper custody and conservation of these materials. One need not criticize this belief system, which was widespread among those working in the field, and has not been seriously criticized throughout the period since the Second World War. In view of the rescue element which was needed, the priorities were probably correct. They should now be reappraised.

4 As time passes and new archival materials become available, the range of subjects for which the archives are primary sources is increased, while at the same time the infrastructural knowledge among the new groups of users is not developed.

5 The use of original materials in school education is still embryonic, and its development has been hindered more by institutional constraints than by user need.

6 Institutional constraints also operate against existing groups of users by restricting opening hours, access facilities, equipment, publicity and the will to improve outreach.

7 The coordination between specialized and national information services and local information services has been poor, or at least patchy. Users in country districts and minor towns have found access to the national systems difficult – in fact impossible without travelling, or access to unusually large funds. Users in major cities have been somewhat better placed, but the services provided by public library systems have been variable, the relationships between library and archive services have been (and still are) very erratic, and there has been much constraint from the general limitation of local government. Academic information services have in many places been even more difficult to access, and constraints imposed by government finance have been powerful here too.

8 There has been no national information plan, or central leadership. Coordination between institutions, services and localities has therefore been eccentric and under-financed. Infrastructural and common facilities which might underlie the development of coordinated services have had little chance to develop.

It is clear that there ought to be systematic examination of the problem of user needs and the response to them. The inquiry should also cover the whole question of information services and supply in neighbourhoods and regions. There is also a technological aspect, for in the long run information supply will no doubt use channels not available at present. French initiatives in teletext probably point the way.

There is no doubt that many new developments, improvements or extensions to archives services have been prevented by lack of resources. It is clear that there is a narrow limit not only to the resources actually committed but also to the resources which could ever conceivably be added to them. Some, probably important, extensions to the service are likely to result from the coordination of different information services in the future. After that we should consider whether it is possible to sustain a professional ethic which would allow refusal of service to some users, or a refusal to extend into some areas of service, because of financial or staffing constraints. Archivists, like others, are used to living within narrow means, but up to now have usually found a way of avoiding too much restriction of service. It would be a strange and hostile world in which it would really be necessary to impose newly devised limits, especially since all the time people are creating new archival materials.

What should an archives and records service be?

The argument so far has been that there should be a move from services based on the management of materials to those designed to provide a service to users. However in practice, traditional approaches to the design of archives and records services have still some validity. A small service can always begin by setting up a records centre or archival repository, collecting materials into them and managing these collections actively. For smaller organizations and perhaps for some local archives services this may remain a viable approach. It would be useful to have an outline of what these services might be.

Aims

The present custom is to write a mission statement, which states the aims of the service briefly, using the language of public relations, and incorporating declarations of high principle. These things are more useful than they might seem, for it is often difficult to stimulate the idealism of either staff or employers. A statement of aims which brings in this element could do good before it becomes quite banal. It is not easy to write one, though, for there are not many good models.

(a) *Territorial*

'The mission of the Borsetshire Record Office is to acquire all the significant archival materials which arose within the county, and collect and make available knowledge about external primary sources of information about the county. We aim to conserve our holdings to the best standard, and to provide a centre of excellence for the advanced study of the county and its people.'

(b) *An in-house records and archives service*

'The mission of the Pecksniff Architectural Group archives service is to discover, manage, conserve and utilize the archival heritage of the organization, in association with the other information services within the group, with the aim of providing a first-class information facility for members of the group and for associated workers in the industry.'

Such statements of aim should of course give an indication of the

20

field within which management would be carried out, or in which acquisitions would be made, and there should be a reference to conservation standards. The most important feature, one which has often been missing in the past, is a reference to the user services to be provided, and to the role which the service is intended to fulfil, the true aim of the archives service insofar as it is an institution in itself.

That the Borsetshire Record Office should see itself as a local institute of historical research, or of local studies, is often assumed, but rarely stated. If it is not stated, then it is likely that the staff and users will not respond to the challenges presented by the actual facts of their operation. If there is an unspoken assumption that in some respects the archives service falls short of the best academic standard applicable, or is somehow not to be judged as a research institute, then the assumption will also be that a less demanding aim has been chosen because the institution is somehow not worthy. Yet it is quite usual to find archives services whose staff do not see themselves or their service as of high academic standing; this perception is often not justified. A clear aim to act as a fully recognized research institution in the chosen area is surely the right one for a regional or local archives service, as well as for specialist repositories. Liaison with the other information services may be a way to strengthen the determination of all concerned to achieve this target.

The nature of the overall aim ought to be directly influential in determining the specific programmes followed. If the mission statement says that the archives service is to be a centre of studies, then there must, of course, be programmes of study, teaching and research. Though it will clearly be necessary for acquisitions of the most important archival material to be achieved first (so that there will be some material basis for the research programme), the academic activities must be given a reasonable priority and status. Without these, a proper balance will not be achieved.

Objectives

The rest of this book is concerned with setting objectives which govern the processes and programmes within the service, covering acquisitions or areas of operation, the conservation of materials and systems, and the development of services to users. The structure of the archives should be consciously designed so as to achieve the targets set out under this heading.

Conclusion

At the beginning of this chapter it was pointed out that every kind of organization had a need to manage information, and that the records and archives services had a place, together with other information services, in this management practice. Since there are very many different kinds of organization in existence, it is not surprising if there are many different kinds of records and archives service. They vary by size, by the nature of the materials on which they concentrate, by whether they work inside the organization or outside it, and by the kind of user service they offer. All these different services are linked together by the fact that their staffs belong (in most cases, consciously) to an organized professional group which is in process of stimulating the setting of standards in many areas of professional life and practice. This book is intended to help in this process, and the rest of it is devoted to a more detailed consideration of some of the main processes and procedures used in records and archives administration.

The management and exploitation of archives is based upon a body of theory, which has resulted in a set of principles or applications widely agreed upon, and realized in working practices. Recent attempts to debunk this body of theory and practical principles have not succeeded in reducing its power in directing professional approaches. We have to recognize that the advent of new information-bearing materials and administrative practices may very well change the character of work in archives, and modify the structure of theory that underlies it. Nevertheless to say that there is no general body of theory is to misunderstand the nature of theory. A theoretical structure underlies every sphere of human activity, and serves to guide it forward into unknown areas of experience. The theory of a professional area is not or should not be rigid or narrowing, but should give the guidelines on which future development and change will be based.

> Librarians are Platonists, who are taught to deal with absolute categories and ideal classifications, whereas archivists are Aristotelians, who think and organise in a relativistic framework. [12]

Notes and references

1 Several short histories of British government archives services and of the PRO exist, and are listed in Evans, F.B. (comp.) ,*The history of archives administration: a select bibliography* Unesco studies in documentation, libraries and archives 6, Paris, 1979, 52-4. See also Cantwell, J.D., *The Public Record Office 1838-1958, HMSO, 1991;* Bond, M., 'The formation of the archives of Parliament, 1497-1691', in Ranger, F. (ed.), *Prisca munimenta: studies in archival and administrative history presented to Dr A.E.J. Hollaender*, University of London Press, 1973, 118-29.

2 *Dictionary of archival terminology: English and French, with equivalents in Dutch, German, Italian, Russian and Spanish*, Walne, P. (ed.), International Council on Archives Handbooks series 3, K.G. Saur, 1984. *Vocabulaire des archives: archivistique et diplomatique contemporaines*, Les dossiers de la normalisation, AFNOR, Paris, 1986.

3 Jenkinson, C.H., *A manual of archive administration*, originally published 1922; quotations in the present work are from the second (revised) edition, ed. R.H. Ellis, Percy Lund Humphries, London, 1965.

4 *op.cit.*, p.4.

5 *op.cit.*, p.11.

6 *op.cit.*, pp.9-10.

7 The case of the Upper Clyde Shipbuilders, 1970-1972 is an example. See National Maritime Museum, *Modern British ship-building: a guide to historical records*, Maritime Monographs and Reports No. 48, 1980, 3-4.

8 Cook, M., *The management of information from archives*, Gower, 1986, 7-8.

9 I am indebted to the manager, Mr Terry Whitehead.

10 For example, by Cook (1986), p.9.

11 Newton, S.C. (ed.), *Office automation and records management*, Society of Archivists, Records Management Group, 1981.

12 Stielow, F.W., 'Archival theory redux and redeemed: definition and context toward a general theory', *The American archivist*, **54**, 1991, 18.

2

Records management

What is records management?

A few years ago the answer to this question was relatively clear. There were two schools of thought. One, based on RM as a management technique, viewed it as a means of increasing efficiency and reducing costs in day-to-day business. The other, the archival school, viewed the management of current records from the standpoint of their ultimate disposal. In practice, there was a reasonably close relationship between these two, and practitioners of both kinds shared a coherent philosophy and body of technical knowledge. This was expressed in a single textbook, published in 1969, by William Benedon.[1] In it, the following definition was offered: 'Records Management ... [is] the direction of a program designed to provide economy and efficiency in the creation, organisation, maintenance, use and retrieval, and disposition of records, assuring that needless records will not be created or kept and valuable records will be preserved and available'.

Records managers who saw their task primarily as an aspect of current management would emphasize those elements of their work that concentrated on economy and efficiency. Those whose point of origin lay in the archives service would emphasize the promotion of good-quality records, and their regular removal from current systems, ultimately into the archives. So a later summary definition could say:

> 'A moderate and practical view of records management ... is that its main concern is the control of the processes whereby records become archives. Withdrawal of non-current records, their handling and storage, and their evaluation as potential archives are the essentials of the subject'.[2]

There is clearly a wide area held in common between these two views, despite the fundamental divergence of underlying aims.

Both schools have since developed quite strongly. Practitioners of the first sort tend to be dominant in North America, and have founded there a system for the certification of records managers which operates today under the umbrella of the Association of Records Managers and Administrators (ARMA) and the Institute of Certified Records Managers (ICRM). The tradition has been much reinforced by two practices in the USA. It is normal there for legislation to require the specific retention of classes of records, and it is also common for official inquiries to investigate the affairs of public or private bodies. These inquiries, and other legal events, usually have the power to enforce the production of records.

Although Europe has seen some increase in legislative or governmental requirements for records, this tradition has made much less progress there, and the American records management tradition, in which the records manager is in certain circumstances seen as dominant over the archivist, has not established itself. Nevertheless, Europe provides a number of strong members of the International Records Management Council, affiliated to the International Council on Archives. This Council's *Bulletin*, founded in 1987, manages to express the views of both schools of thought.

The archival approach to RM, more characteristic of Britain, has also developed. Many local authority record offices have established posts of the anomalously named archivist for 'modern records', whose duty basically it is to arrange the orderly transfer of non-current records into the archives. Groups of archivists interested in this aspect were sufficiently influential as long ago as 1968 to stimulate the beginning of a series of seminars under the aegis of the Society of Archivists, and these eventually developed into the Records Management Group within the Society.[3] The RMG has sustained a regular and consistent programme of activities since about 1977.

A third school of thought is now in process of establishing itself. A number of (mainly young) records managers formed the Records Management Society of Great Britain in 1983. This event signalled a number of new developments.

There have been several important new publications. Two new textbooks bid to replace Benedon's, which is now hard to obtain,[4] and there are new journals. At least one specialist consultancy firm,

Task Force Pro Libra (TFPL), has accepted RM as a major programme area. Other new activities and training programmes can be seen. The new group of activists is much more involved in the current management of businesses than the members of the archive-based group have tended to be; their standpoint tends to be that RM forms part of the broader discipline of information management and, like it, should use all the technical skills available to managers.

A seminar on training for RM, held in 1990, brought to light a growing sense of division between the current management and the archival approaches to RM. That there is an important difference between the two is a view shared by the present author and this book is written consciously to represent the interests of archivists working in RM, and not those of a records manager or information manager standing centrally in the discipline. However, even so, it is clear that archival RM must be deeply influenced by the current state of the art, and by the development of RM towards information management.

Many archivist records managers have always been conscious of the basic principles in this new movement. They have seen, for example, that the material which is the subject of RM has always been information rather than physical records, and that the well-being of the whole organization is affected by the efficiency of its recording procedures.

This discussion allows us to proceed to a definition which will support a statement of overall aim and a specification of the concepts of RM. Records management is a discipline which aims:

(a) to understand and control the information collected or generated by an organization, so that

(b) all appropriate information required for the conduct of business is acquired, made available to the people who need it, and recorded in suitable systems, and

(c) the most valuable core of the resulting records is exploitable in the long term.

The convergences and changes of emphasis which are implicit in this statement are summarized in a recent international publication.[5]

It is assumed that the archives service of any organization will also have an important stake in all the operations covered by the statement, and will also subscribe to the overall aims (often set out as a 'mission statement') of the organization itself. In a private firm, these aims will be commercial, and it is not surprising, therefore, that there is a great difference between the attitudes to be found in a public service organization and those of an RM unit in the private sector, even though both are aimed at supporting the efficiency of the administrative structure. Information management must always be practised in the first place for the benefit of the creating organization; any secondary values generated by it must remain to some extent in the background, however important they may ultimately be.

Information management

Records are 'any information captured in reproducible form that is required for conducting business'.[6] From this point of view, records are seen less as series of material objects, and more as components in dynamic systems. These systems, taken together, constitute the main management activity of an organization.

It is always a good thing to be aware of the difference between records as objects and the systems in which the objects are generated and stored. Many of the instruments of control used in RM can be used in either of these two different ways, to control the information systems, or to control the movement of documents. The ability to work in these two ways is a strength, a useful technique. Records managers should know in which way they are operating at any given moment – whether controlling the system which contains information, or disposing of the items on which the information is written. The essential task of a records manager is to control the ways in which information is stored and used: 'ways' here means both systems and the documents within the systems.

By contrast, information management is much less constrained by the need to handle objects. Information itself is not material, it is an abstract commodity which takes real form only when captured and put on to a carrier. Information can come from any source, and belongs to a universe of knowledge which also is not constrained by the physical nature of the administration. An information manager should be conscious of this universe of knowledge, and the sector of it which is directly relevant to the business in hand. The problem then is to make sure that the whole organization is open to receive it. The work includes not only capturing information and setting up access facilities, but also providing for the education of users. This is a far-ranging set of activities which affects and is affected by all aspects of the life of the employing authority.

Information technology is relevant and useful both to records management and to information management, but in different ways. To the records manager, IT is linked closely with recording systems, and individual records can be held and processed by it. IT can also be a tool for making records available, and for controlling them. To the information manager, IT has wider uses, in communications, in providing links with information sources, in user education and in helping to structure the whole administration.

Information management and RM are clearly linked closely together. It is even possible to confuse them, although information management has wider areas of action. For example, collecting data for statistical reports, making these reports available to decision-makers and writing them into documents, are information activities which are outside traditional RM. So too is managing the library and documentation services, which carry information and materials bought in from outside the organization. (Records and recording systems are essentially generated from within.) Despite these differences, it is important to recognize the link between information and records management, because (a) it creates a state of mind which is dynamic and concerned with the intellectual control of processes within the industry; and (b) it facilitates the integration of a number of different information-based services.

RM at the present day remains essentially a discipline which concentrates on controlling and exploiting the media (not necessarily, but mainly, paper) which carry information. It is likely, perhaps certain, that the discipline will change as electronic methods come to dominate administration. This stage has not yet been reached, at least in most organizations, but it is probably necessary for most records managers to consider the early planning stages of the new systems.

RM is a discipline which will stand on its own quite easily. In fact, it is one which is likely to flourish in a severely constricted financial climate, for it emphasizes economy and maximizes effective service. It is also a discipline which should be understood by archivists, for the two are end-on to each other, and institutional archives cannot be complete without an RM component.

The range and content of an RM programme

An outline training syllabus

The Unesco RAMP study published as a guideline for training in archive and records management in 1982[7] sets out an area of work in which records managers (especially those based in archives) should be able to show competence.

In this analysis, RM is one of four core professional subjects: RM, archives administration, interpretative sciences and administrative history. The two last of these subjects are marked 'as appropriate', so that in international terms the two dominant subjects are RM and archives administration. It is clear that candidates for entry to the profession should accept that RM forms an essential part of archival training.

This proposition is accepted in practice by training courses in archives established in Britain. Acceptance of the principle has consequences in defining the type of candidate who should be attracted and admitted to courses: they should be willing to enter into situations where the current well-being of their employing organization is a primary value. They should be able to see themselves as participating in their employer's industry.

The actual content of the RM part of the training course outlined in the guidelines is structured as follows:

1 *Design and organization of an RM programme*
   (a) This deals with the range of responsibility to be under-taken over the records: the concept of life-cycle control of records, compared with the concept of more limited control.
   (b) The relationships between operating departments in the employing organization, the archives and RM services.

2 *Records creation*
   (a) Methods of generating correspondence; the use of staff in these services; automation (for example, management of word-processing facilities).
   (b) The management of administrative directives, circulars and instructions; writing technical manuals for directing and training staff.
   (c) The design and use of forms as a management tool.
   (d) Reports management (including the introduction and control of text processing and creating management information systems for departmental executives – some knowledge of statistical techniques would be useful here).
   (e) Mail management: controlling the flow of inward, outward

and internal documentation, and setting up methods of servicing the decision-makers.

3 *Records maintenance and use*
   (a) Filing classification systems; analysis of functions and the topics which derive from them; classification schemes and the vocabulary control that goes with them.
   (b) Management of filing systems (including the use of technical means for recording, storage and retrieval of information, involving microforms, video recording, automated indexes etc.).
   (c) Filing equipment and supplies.
   (d) Office machines, including copying machines, and control of supplies.
   (e) The management of office space and equipment.
   (f) The design and control of central microfilm services (which may be linked to a vital records programme).

4 *Records disposal*
   (a) Records surveys and setting up schedules to control the disposal or retention of records.
   (b) Records centre management:
      Planning and administration; staffing and costing the service;
      Input of records;
      Reference service based on the records centre.

5 *Specialized areas*
   (a) Paperwork quality control programmes.
   (b) Clerical work measurement.
   (c) Source data automation.
   (d) Automated and electronic data processing management.
   (e) The management of micrographics systems.
   (f) Documentation programmes; making sure the right information is obtained, and that it is available where it is needed.
   (g) Training Departmental Records Officers, records staff, and all staff that are to handle records or share in information services.

6 *Programme evaluation*
   (a) Surveys and evaluation both of departmental paperwork operations and of departmental records management programmes.

(b)   Professional ethics and standards.

The guideline was tested internationally both before and after publication. It ought to be possible to regard it as an agreed standard for the range of training required for a general practitioner in RM. An analysis of it shows that it insists that records managers (viewed in the context of archival training) should:

- have an approach which starts from the concept of the life-cycle of records (records managers should be concerned with records at every stage from generation to disposal – from cradle to grave, as the common phrase has it)
- be trained in at least the most common methods of generating and processing records
- be able to manage traditional records centre operations;
- regard automation as a tool rather than as an all-embracing environment.

This kind of training would produce archivists who can use the techniques of RM not only to the benefit of their employing organization, but also to the benefit of the archives. It does not seem ignoble to accept that the creation of an archive is actually one of the minor aims of an organization, or that it is right and necessary for archivists to take an active part in the organization's current work. Both of these complementary principles are the source of life, energy and good ideas among archivists.

The training outline gives a possible structure for a wide range of RM operational programmes. Records managers may be able to choose from this range, to suit their particular circumstances. All varieties of RM, however, operate by constructing and using a set of databases.

Creating a working database: the retention schedule

The central database in any RM system is generally termed the *retention schedule*. This contains a list of all classes of record used by the administration, together with relevant facts about them (bulk, rate of accrual, legal significance, disposal, etc.).[8] A retention schedule is often compiled as a result of a systematic survey.

Surveys have many uses, but the principal outcome is the creation of a database which will be the main tool of management. Records managers can hardly exercise their responsibility until they know the

Dept:	Section:	
Admin	Financial	Legal

Figure 2.1 Initial appraisal decisions

field they are operating in. The working database consists essentially of two tables, one of record systems, the other of record classes.

The register of record systems is the more difficult to create, maintain and use. Yet unless it exists in some form, it will not be possible to manage or evaluate any of the work processes set up in the organization.

Creating a schedule of classes should be easier. The survey findings include a list of all classes encountered, setting them in their administrative context. Sorting the survey worksheets into classes within sections, within departments, should provide a full list. The next step is to apply appraisal tests.

From an RM standpoint, there are four considerations in records appraisal: administrative, financial, legal and research. The first step is to get opinions on the first three of these. The class description can be copied on to a card or computer file which contains a box for each of the values indicated. Experienced records managers will be able to write in an initial recommendation as to retention and disposal. This will be based on their experience in this and other organizations, their knowledge of information sources inside it and outside, their knowledge of research processes, again inside and outside, and research they have carried out themselves. A note on research values should be provided by archivists or records managers.

Opinions on administrative values can then be sought from management, on financial values from the internal audit unit or treasury, and legal values from the legal services department. When all opinions are in, the best is chosen (generally this means taking the opinion which offers the longest retention, although there are no doubt exceptions). The draft retention schedule can then be drawn up as a unitary document, and circulated for more comment.

It is always necessary to maintain the retention schedule and issue revised versions every time there is a major reshuffle of departmental structures (which nowadays is usually quite frequent).

New classes are constantly being created. The records management staff should watch for these and get them incorporated in the retention schedule as quickly as possible.

Retention schedules list every class under departmental and section headings, and allocate to each a lifespan and a disposal instruction. Some retention schedules keep this information as simple as possible and do not include provision for moving the records from one storage area to another. The most elaborate examples, however, do include this information. Thus a maximum entry for one class could be as here:

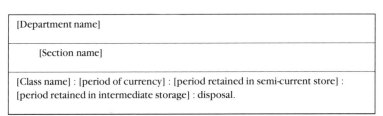

[Department name]
[Section name]
[Class name] : [period of currency] : [period retained in semi-current store] : [period retained in intermediate storage] : disposal.

Figure 2.2 Retention schedule entry

Finally, the schedule should be adopted and authorized as a formal expression of the policy of the organization. The RM service will probably wish to print it and make copies widely available.

The retention schedule is a document which lays down the organization's policy on the disposal of all classes. Making it often involves conscious policy decisions: for example, to retain the records of mechanical processes (e.g. machine logs) for 12 months, and then destroy them; or to retain personnel files for 12 years after the retirement or death of the staff member concerned. Policy may have to change in regard to particular classes as the result of new legislation or risk assessments, and the records managers should advise on this, and be ready with the necessary amendments at the proper time.

One of the tasks which the retention schedule carries out is to identify records which can be classified as vital to the survival of the organization. If there is an unexpected catastrophe, such as a fire or flood, which destroys current or recent records, it is still possible to rescue the main work and life of the organization, provided that these vital records can be recovered in some form. The retention schedule should indicate which they are, and there should be provision for

Department code
Class name   System name   Class reference number
Abstract (summarizes informational content of the class)   (free text)
Summary of use of the class in the department
Date coverage

Bulk (storage occupied at the date of the survey)
 	
     Storage equipment used
 	
     Form/type/genre of materials
 	
     Cost by category

Legal provisions affecting the class
Financial/audit provisions affecting the class

Retention recommendation
     (Process of securing assent to the operation of this)
     Authority for disposal

Vital records categorization
 	
Retirement of non-current materials from the current system
     Semi-current/non-current components
     Selection criteria/method
 	
Finding aids

Notes; special features   Cross-references to allied classes

Figure 2.3 The structure of an RM database

keeping them, or copies, in a safe place. This work can be coordinated with a disaster plan.

Because it enshrines central policy in these matters it is a document (or rather a database) of general interest in the organization. This view, if presented to lay members of an organization, might cause some surprise. If it does, this would be an indication that there has been a failure to present the proper scope and role of RM. Records managers would do well to seek all possible means to keep the schedule available for consultation by, and present to the conscious-ness of, departmental staff. In manual systems, this would involve keeping updated copies easily available in all filing centres, and with the secretaries of all senior managers. They should be available for all induction and in-house training schemes. In an automated adminis-tration, a better way is to make it one of the databases held in the central email system, so that it can be called up by any department which wishes to transfer, create or otherwise vary the treatment of records.

The full structure of the database which serves as a central tool for information management through records control, is outlined in Figure 2.3.

The plan: what is the programme to do?

When survey and analysis work is complete, it is possible to design an RM programme, and the information management programme of which it is a part, with some precision.

RM is to do with the management of records and recording systems, and by extension of the information held in them. There is nothing in the theory which makes it necessary for records managers to secure physical control of the records. Intellectual, or manage-ment, control is all that is necessary. However, it is normally accepted that successful RM programmes do incorporate an element of physical control, and it is usually on the operation of this physical control that costing exercises are carried out. Physical control is always easier to perceive and evaluate, and it is not surprising that RM's most obvious public face should be the one which is most often noted by the laity. Physical control of records is done by setting up and running a records centre, or intermediate store.

RECORDS TRANSFERRED TO RECORDS CENTRE	
Part I: Data sheet	Consignment
Originating dept	
	Date
General description of records class (continue on separate sheets)	
Storage accommodation cleared Filing cabinets Transfer boxes Shelving Cubic footage of records transferred	
Recommendations for retention	
Classified confidential/unrestricted	
Transferred by	

Figure 2.4 A transfer list incorporating levels of description

Part II: Transfer list

			Consignment	
Originating dept			Page	
				Records centre use

Ref. no.	Title/description	Span dates	Action date	Location

37

Input of records

The function of a records centre is to store, and provide a base for the exploitation of, all the records which (a) are judged to be suitable for retention beyond a given (short) period after the end of their current life; and (b) can be retired systematically from current systems.

The procedures for transferring these records to the records centre should be the subject of a user education programme. Many organizations find it useful to design and circulate a brochure which explains the purpose and value of their records centre, and gives instructions on how to go about using it.

There are two fundamental rules.

1 All records brought to the records centre should be accompanied by finding aids.
2 No record should be admitted to the records centre unless it has been appraised, and given a date for the next action.

Finding aids

It has been customary in the past for records managers to require originating departments to write out the finding aids which are to accompany records being transferred to the records centre. This is done by issuing a supply of blank 'transfer lists' to be completed by the originating office, together with simple instructions. Figure 2.4 is an example of a transfer list.

The transfer list is intended to act as the basic finding aid, by which any item in the transferred records can be retrieved and brought into use. Experience has shown (a) that very often a more careful description is needed than any that the originating office is likely to provide; (b) that additional finding aids, such as indexes or computerized systems, are also needed, and with these some vocabulary control may be useful; and (c) there may be a need for additional control instruments.

Depth of description

A more carefully constructed description is required in two ways. More obviously, the wording used in writing item descriptions in Part II of the transfer list must be such as will satisfactorily identify the material, even to those who are not familiar with the original recording system. To someone familiar, a description such as 'flimsy thirds', or 'the grey folders' may be significant; but after the lapse of some time, a more formal description of the actual content of the material is probably needed. This problem could be solved by a good and well-sustained programme of user education, and by closely supervising the actual transfer of records. The second problem is more difficult.

Additional finding aids

It is necessary to have regard to the archival levels of arrangement, even in the case of ephemeral records transferred for a short period before destruction. The terms used in archival levels of arrangement are explained in Chapter 3. Many RM systems in the past have set out

			Level
Group: General Manager's Office, Home Division			2
Subgroup:	Internal administration section		2.5
	Established 1984 to administer property and		
	manufacturing operations in the Panbridge area. Many		
	records transferred from the former Home		
	Administration Division, which was closed in the same		
	year.		
RGF	Research grant award files	1984-1986	3
1	Medical Research Council 100654		4
2	JG Parkinson & Co, special grant		4
3	Save the Children, additional, 85/344		4
MIR	Materials inspection reports	1990-1991	3
1	Eastern works, 1st quarter		4
2	Eastern works, 2nd quarter		4
COR	General correspondence	1960-1980	3
/32	Complaints, A–G, 1960-5		4
/104	Road diversions, Panbridge, 1968		4

Note: Level numbers relate to MAD2 standard, which is explained in Chapter 3.

Level 2	Group
Level 2.5	Subgroup
Level 3	Class
Level 4	Item

Figure 2.5 Example of a multi-level description

to control materials only at item level, listing individual file titles or case numbers in the equivalent of Part II of the transfer list. Realizing the shortcomings of this approach, an attempt was made to introduce a group or subgroup list.[9] This is the main reason why Part I of the transfer list was introduced. We can now see that there is a need for still further information, this time at class level. The example on the previous page shows why.

This list shows how useful the division into levels is. In particular, it shows the value of listing at class level – represented in the example by the entries coded RGF, MIR and COR. For many purposes the class title and the relevant date are sufficient for retrieval, especially where the client is expecting to search for particular files or for particular papers within a file. It is not good or efficient practice to repeat class titles for every item description within them. Therefore there must be provision on the transfer list for these class headings, and a way must be found to train clerical staff to understand what they are and how to use them.

Additional control instruments

The transfer lists are the first and most central of the records centre finding aids, but some others must be derived from them, to help with administering the system.

It may be useful to maintain a *register of consignments*. This would record the receipt of quantities of records transferred from each department, giving a total of the storage space occupied. Records routinely destroyed are also recorded and the total space deducted. Records managers should be able to say how much of their space is occupied, and for how long, by the records of any given department. This information is needed for planning, and also for costing and (if necessary) charging out the expenses of the service.

Many RM services use *box labels*. These are sometimes used as the main means of physical control of materials in the records centre. There is a consensus, however, that the loss of security that this method entails is a serious drawback. If boxes are labelled in such a way as to indicate to passers-by what kinds of record are inside them, the possibility of a breach of security is always there. It is a better practice simply to have a call number or location code visible on the outside of record containers. Even so, a box label generated by the system can be useful if it is seen as a box index, showing only minimal information. A duplicate can be kept in secure conditions in the records centre office. Copies can be kept in different orders: shelf location order, action date order, consignment order. In automated systems, all of these sortings should be able to be provided by the computer-held database.

Retrieval and issue of records: information service

The whole point of a records centre is that by establishing physical control over the materials transferred to it, records managers may be able to improve the provision of information from them. If the records centre cannot provide this service, its only justification would be that storage there was more economical than storage in office space. Economies of this type are usually possible, it is true, and are sometimes spectacular; but the cost situation has to be calculated in each case.

Firstly, there should be ground rules about the way requests for records and for information are to be handled. In central government and in large-scale business RM, there is a tradition that (a) records are only issued to the departments which transferred them (which are their 'owners', in a commonly used phrase); and (b) user demands are met by the issue of specified records. Both of these assumptions should be questioned.

The principle that records 'belong' to the departments which created them, or at least which held them at the time when they were transferred to intermediate storage, is difficult to justify. RM programmes work best if it is explicitly acknowledged that records created in the course of business are the property of the overall organization, and can be disposed of in accordance with its rules, drawn up in association with records managers.

Thus in British central government, documents created in the course of government business are declared to be Public Records, and subject to rules derived from the Public Records Acts. That this is the legal situation does not prevent government departments from making arrangements for the disposal and use of their records, but it does give the Public Record Office the status, for some purposes, of an executing agency. The law of ownership and control can be used to support systems for the protection and use of the material.

Similar rules rarely exist in non-government agencies, but where they do, they can give the RM programme a useful stiffening. What is to be avoided is a situation where a department, or even an individual office-holder, can operate as if records produced in the course of business were the property of that department or office-holder. Records should be exploited to the benefit of the organization as a whole.

Nevertheless, in practice, a rule that prevents the records centre from issuing records to anyone other than the transferring department (at least in the first place) may often be useful in an RM system. It is necessary to secure the trust and collaboration of creating or transferring departments if RM is to work successfully. The security of their records and information is a most important consideration, to which records managers must give their best attention. The larger the organization, the more likely it is that departments will wish to control who has access to information from their records.

As against this, research is nowadays an essential tool of management. The decision-makers who are responsible for the success or failure of the organization as a whole must be able to secure the best information about the current situation and past experience. Records managers are an important group of information providers, and they should be able to collate, supply and organize information from the records so that it can be presented usefully to senior management. A records service which did not do this would not be serving its paymasters well.

Records managers who are responsible for providing particular records on request are carrying a considerable degree of responsibility. The records in question may have a good deal of practical importance – they may, for example, prove or fail to prove ownership of financial or real property, or support the pension rights of groups of people. Keeping track of individual records in the great mass held in a records centre is not simple. There may be practical reasons, especially in a very large organization, for keeping records managers' responsibilities at this level. Much greater is the responsibility of records managers who provide actual substantive information, drawn from the records, for the use of operating departments or of senior management.

Records managers who provide information directly must have the necessary skills. At the very least, they must be able to compose reports which correctly base their factual statements on the relevant sources. It may be that they will have to be trained in statistical techniques. This has not been traditional in RM, but must become so.

42

These records managers will not only be able to answer questions like 'what do we know about...?', but will also proactively supply information in reports on particular subjects to relevant individuals in senior management. In principle, the sources of information need not be restricted to internal ones. Information may often be obtained from exterior sources as well as from the records or from the observation of practice. Care should be taken, though, not to fall into an old trap, which is to ignore internal sources and rely on external ones. Organizations which neglect RM usually manage to get their working information externally. It is a central principle of RM that much or most information required for management purposes is actually available from internal sources, if only these were properly organized.

Therefore, information can be seen as a valuable commodity which can be used as a central resource, and as a basis for research which benefits the whole organization.

Information service: practicalities

The actual retrieval of records from the records centre, and the control of their issue and return involve some techniques.

Transfer lists provide the initial and basic finding aids. Hence the accuracy with which they are completed and the language used in them are important. The top copies of the transfer lists are usually filed in order of receipt, by departments. The departments which transferred the records also hold a copy, in which location and disposal information has been written in, and they too will therefore have a file of transfer lists. This means that they can ask for any record and give its location.

However, departments may not be as well organized as this, or they may have an enquiry which demands information rather than specific records as an answer. To meet this situation, some sort of access point must then be provided by the records centre staff. Traditionally, and in manual systems, this has been by constructing an index to the transfer list information. Nowadays, it would be more likely that computers will be used to store, sort and search the data from the transfer lists.

Records withdrawn from the store and issued to administrative users must be controlled. In manual systems, this is usually done by recording the issue in two places: the central control point (records centre office), and the place of location of the record. The central record forms a file of 'records out', which may be used to provide statistics and to check timely returns. At the place of location, the marker should be distinctive, carry the date of issue on it, and should be fastened in a place on the shelves, or on the outside of the box, where it can be seen from the end of the row of shelves. Records staff can therefore check on records issued either by consulting the take-out slips stored centrally in their office, or by walking through the storage area.

It is a common practice for records staff to attach a sticker to the front of any record which has been issued by the records centre. Stickers carry an eye-catching message that the record has been supplied by the RM system and should be returned. There should also be a space for the location code, so that when it does come back, the records staff know where it should go, and that it is not a new accession. Tracking the stickers is a rough-and-ready way of counting the number of times records have been issued from a given class. This piece of information is useful in appraisal – for example, when reviewing – and is difficult to learn if the system has not been automated.

Traditionally, RM systems have not always included provision for chasing up records issued and not returned for long periods. After all, if records are taken out by administrators who feel that they need them ready to hand for a long time, that is a decision within the competence of the originating department. However, it is a good practice to send out reminders. Records are often kept out because of neglect, and they often get lost because one official has passed a file on to another. The system should provide resources for collecting data on records which have not been returned within, say, three months, and sending reminders round to the user departments. Once again, computers have proved very useful for this kind of routine management task.

Provision of information from the records includes the possibility of giving access to them on site. There may be an argument for providing reading-room accommodation in the records centre. This would certainly be justified if there were many cases of access by external (authorized) researchers. In other cases, representatives of user departments might have to have facilities for searching their holdings directly on the shelves. This is not a desirable practice where random-access storage is employed, but it may be necessary. These searchers will have to be accompanied and supported by records centre staff, because of the difficulty of identifying particular locations, as well as because of security problems.

Costing records services

It is possible to put a cost on all RM activities. In fact it is a basic principle that all managers should be able to provide information on the cost of every aspect of their work. This principle of course applies also to the management of the user departments. In organizations where this is done, it should be possible to compare the costs of the RM service and the costs of record-related activities in the departments. The RM programme should, of course, show a net saving.

In all cases, there are activities within the organization which cannot be costed, but which must be evaluated in other terms. For RM, the most important such cost is that of providing information proactively. There is no way of avoiding this difficulty. The evaluation of RM should include some kind of survey of user opinion. If it is working well, there will be a detectable degree of user satisfaction, and a general willingness to use the service.

It is fashionable now to expect services to operate on a competitive costed-out basis. Records managers should welcome this, if their service is well designed, and the setting for it reasonably favourable. Costs can be worked out on a realistic basis, and compared with the costs of alternative arrangements.

The cost of the service offered by central storage in a records centre would be reckoned on these factors:

- storage per cubic metre per annum
- retrieval per document, including routine replacement
- issuing reminders
- answering record-based enquiries
- disposal of records per cubic metre.

Departmental managers faced with the need to pay these charges have three alternatives to consider:

1 Retaining records in their departments, and servicing them by their own departmental staff. The cost of this will in many cases be higher. The cost of space in a working office is by definition higher than the cost of space in a high-density, low-cost store. Staff time has to be taken from what is available for the central

activity of the department. Staff are usually not trained in information work. It is always likely that the quality of the service obtained will be unacceptably low.

2 Reorganizing records creation and use on site, so as to improve economies of storage, and the effective retrieval of information from minimal recording. But these are functions of RM. If they have not been done under the aegis of a central RM programme, then it is right that departments should indeed undertake such RM activities on their own. Every organization of any size needs RM, and will often find ways to provide it one way or another.

3 Using the services of a commercial records management firm. If the circumstances of the internal RM are right, it should hardly be possible for the internal records centre to be more expensive than an external one, which has to make a profit in the open market. In recent cases where commercial RM has won contracts from internal services, the reason has been that the internal service had been given unsuitable and unnecessarily expensive accommodation: in other words, the fault lay not in the RM service but in the overall management of the organization's buildings. In any case, if commercial service is cheaper, but still efficient, then it may be regarded as a correct RM decision to choose this method. Non-commercial considerations, such as the security of information or the need for positive supply of information to senior management, should also be borne in mind.[10]

On the other hand, it is possible for records managers to consider using any spare capacity for offering an RM service to external bodies on a commercial basis. There is certainly no principle against this. The RM staff of course must take their professional ethic seriously in protecting the security of their clients' records and information.

A properly costed and suitably resourced RM service should have no fear of failing the economic test. In accounting terms it ought to provide considerable savings for its host organization. This is because records storage is a significant factor in administrative costs everywhere. All complex organizations spend a large proportion of their income on records generation and storage. The larger the organization, the more serious is this burden. The purpose of RM is to reduce these costs and improve the efficiency of the information held. Generally, the margins of operation are so wide that it is difficult for even the least ambitious records managers to avoid making significant cost savings.

But, after all, the evaluation of a service should be done on the basis of the real, and not only of the monetary, advantages that it offers. The real advantages of an effective RM programme are that the organization can work well, that employees can relate to each other comfortably, and have the tools they need, that the necessary information is kept and is usable, that the organization can feel that it has an identity, and that it can call upon its past experience as a resource. These things do not feature in the budget, but they are absolutely necessary to success. Costing techniques can be a useful way of comparing methods and measuring success, but they are not the most essential thing.

Automation of RM

Organizations today intend to transfer their administrative systems to electronic media. Some have already achieved this. A fully automated administration demonstrates some quite new features, and will demand a new approach from records managers. The design of systems must incorporate appraisal, and a technological means must be included for archiving databases. Electronic records do not have fixed material formats or carriers, but are assembled technologically in the form in which they are desired for use. This change in the nature of records means that some traditional principles of archival operation must be reassessed. It also means that the active intervention of records managers in the design process is made increasingly necessary. There are technical manuals already in existence to guide this work, and the present book does not attempt to deal with the subject in detail.

The processes outlined earlier in this chapter are set out as manual procedures. As with all procedures, it is not difficult to transpose them to a computer. Transfer lists, for example, can be input to a computer database, and in this form can be much more easily manipulated. The database can be searched to find references to a particular topic, sections of it can be extracted, sorted into different orders, etc. Records whose action date has arrived can be identified; locations can be listed and allocated.

However, this use of computers is still intermediate. Data capture is still manual: the transfer lists are still written out by the transferring department, and the data on them input to the computer by the RM staff, as a separate operation. It must be possible to devise a more radically automated process, to operate in an environment where automated processes are the rule.

A possible next step might be a programme which can be run under a single relational database management system. This might contain files as follows:

> List of record-producing offices
> *Retention schedule/register of classes
> *Consignments register
>> Analysis of holdings/bulk/accrual rate
>> *Charging out
>> Allocation of locations
> *Transfer list: list of items
>> *Disposal notification
>> *Review reports
>> *Disposal record
>> *Issue and return control
>> Box labels
> Inventories of material transferred to archives

At least those elements marked with an asterisk could with advantage be shared with the transferring departments. Some of the databases could generate useful information automatically. Allocation of locations could be done where the system knows what boxes have been disposed of. The issue and return system could generate and circulate overdue notices. Box labels could be printed directly from the transfer list (but should contain a minimum of information, for security reasons).

In an environment where email and electronic communications have become general, these databases could be made part of the common information base in the system. The RM programme could then genuinely move towards full automation.

If departments could inspect the retention schedule online (or at least their own section of it), they could use it to arrange the retirement of non-current records from their system. They could also, if permitted, enter new classes and so help to maintain the schedule; but this would have to be closely supervised by records managers. When records were to be transferred to the records centre, the electronic communication system, using formatted screens, could be used to supply the transfer list information. The resulting database, with records centre information on action date and location, would then be available for departmental staff. They could use another formatted screen to request records from the records centre, and the issue would be recorded until the record was returned. Costs could be allocated, in large part automatically. Records managers would be able to control the whole system, which works together admirably.

In a situation like this there would be a need for considerable education programmes. Secretarial and clerical staff in departments would have to learn skills which are at present largely ignored in training for office skills, concerning the use and disposition of records. Records managers' daily concerns would shift from the management of records centres and the services based on these, to the more general concerns of running organization-wide information flows, and training of departmental staff. There would be considerable advantages in better control, including the control of costs. In ideal situations, most organizations would gain greatly from the ready access to recorded information which would result.

However, even this more integrated database approach still assumes that the most important documentation will be on paper, or other forms of hard copy such as microfilm. The databases are still aimed at controlling records which are carried by media that can be handled, moved about and kept in a physical store. At present, this is the situation in probably the majority of organizations; and there are of course some which will always operate in this way. It is likely that most larger organizations will shortly move their administrations on to an entirely electronic basis. The integrated database approach will spread over the whole field of operation. In automated administrations of this kind the work of records managers must be more central, and must involve active involvement in the design of systems.

Organizations may experience the impact of automation in one of two ways. The new technologies may be introduced centrally as a conscious act. This creates an environment which is inherently favourable to records managers, for their participation in the management of information storage and disposal is much needed. The other way is when there is little or no guidance from central planning, and information technology gains its foothold from below.

Central planning

An automated administration works on sets of databases which relate to each other. These databases deal with:

     finance: receipts
          payroll
          expenditure
     policy development and decision-making
          committee servicing
     communications: external, internal
     staffing
     legal services
     property: acquisition
          maintenance
     process control: acquisition of materials
          procedures
          disposal of materials

Managing a system like this introduces a number of new principles. The most important one, overall, is the concept that information is no longer to be thought of as data carried by particular bits of physical media. In such a system, information has become something held electronically in a system, and subject to constant change. It can only be produced in a form which can be recognized and handled, by causing some sort of output. There will still be a need for (a) documents, carrying data of legal import, and (b) specific data outputs which are used for external actions. To ensure that this is possible, records managers (by whatever name) must clearly be involved in the planning stage. The questions they must ask concern the relationships between the different databases, the interest of various users, legal restrictions on data content and on access, and the long-term implications.

There are three points in the planning of an integrated electronic system where the concerns of RM are of particular importance. These are as follows:

- establishing hardware standards
- establishing software standards
- planning the use of telecommunications.

All three of these demonstrate the need for a discipline that will operate over the whole administration, considered centrally and enforced strongly. (In practice, many organizations in other ways regarded as reasonably disciplined, have failed to establish this one.) The design and purchase of computers and other hardware must conform to the agreed standards, or there will be a failure, compounded over time, to achieve integration. Hardware chosen must not only be compatible over the whole area of the employing organization but must be capable of being sensibly upgraded when new equipment becomes available.

Software compatibility must also include the possibility of being upgraded. The need for compatibility is in itself sufficiently obvious. If one branch or department chooses Word*Star as its word processor, and another chooses Word Perfect, it will be necessary to set up formal interfaces between them. As we move towards Open Systems Interface (OSI), and new operating systems must be chosen, the need for coordinated planning becomes more obvious.

Fortunately in this field, some international standards are becoming available, and more are being designed. Standards like ASCII and ISO 8211 can be built into the system design.

Communications is the newest element in computing, and one whose long-term implications are least appreciated. The transfer of data from one database to another, to have relational effects, is probably the most difficult aspect for RM. Email is developing in two directions. It gives a channel of easy and informal communication between staff, and it also provides a channel for formal and document-based communication. The informal channel is better, more efficient and rapid than the telephone, an annoying and inefficient channel from which we have suffered for four generations. The growing use of informal email will reduce the importance of many kinds of traditional document: memos, letters, office notes. It will also transform the relationship between grades of staff. For example, there may cease to be a clerical/secretarial class whose main task is the translation of written or spoken words into typescript. These workers can then begin to undertake more substantive jobs directed towards the aims of the employing institution. Even documents of legal import can be put together and transmitted electronically and may cease to be unique.

In this changing world, the influence of records managers should be directed towards establishing standards. They should be concerned that information capture, recording, transmission and output should be unimpeded over the organization. It is their responsibility to ensure that information can migrate successfully to new systems when they arrive. They should ensure that the right documents are produced to support the work of the organization in regard to the working of the law, audit and public relations. They should see that there is an adequate output to the archive.

To do all this is to be an effective and clearthinking planner. It does not involve more than a modicum of technical knowledge, which can usually be acquired on the job. It does involve immersion in the immediate management concerns of the organization. In an electronic environment, RM has to be at the centre of senior management decision-making, or it cannot succeed.

Technology from below

Common today are organizations in which IT has been introduced as a result of initiatives from within departments. Individual members of staff, or individual offices and departments, have bought personal computers and set up local systems: 'the expansion of end-user computing in which users control when and how microcomputers are used .... The tools of end-user computing – word processing, spread sheets, electronic mail, and database management systems – help create a highly decentralised work environment that makes it difficult, if not impossible, to support records management as it is generally practised today.'[11]

This is probably a more common situation than the one where technological development is initiated from the centre, and receives its impulse from above. The problems for RM are more serious in a decentralized environment than in a centralized one. When the development has not gone too far, records managers can carry out surveys to find out what databases are being produced, and their specifications in terms of hardware and software. As time passes, local networks appear and systems form themselves into groups. Questions of compatibility and the need to migrate databases into new systems become pressing. Records managers are necessarily associated with the central adoption of standards, and they can hardly abandon this position without losing all power to act progressively and not simply reactively. There is a danger that the RM system itself might become one of several incompatible systems within the organization.

In large organizations where the departments are relatively

autonomous (as in government), the role of RM might be to establish hardware and software standards to support the most fundamental information-gathering and storage functions. An example of how this might work is provided by the plan produced by the Public Record Office for dealing with electronic records generated within government departments. A standard for storing records on optical digital disk was chosen and details of it circulated. Where datasets were appraised and selected for archival retention, they had to be migrated into the agreed format, and transferred in this way. This is a policy for transferring material from current systems into the archives, but it also offers a model for RM at earlier stages in the currency of records. It underlines the close association between RM and general and technical standards.

Despite a recognition that information held within a system can be considered independently of the disposition of the media it is carried on, RM seems inseparable from measures for that disposition. Information in itself is too volatile to be held; it slips through the fingers. If records managers concentrate on developing systems for recording and using types of information, and then on transferring the content of those systems to usable storage, they will continue to contribute importantly to the life of organizations.

Notes and references

1 Benedon, W., *Records management*, originally published in New Jersey, 1969; reprint by Trident Bookshop, California. The quotation is from p. 258.
2 Cook, M., *Archives administration*, Dawson Publishing, 1977, 25.
3 Cook, M., McDonald, L.J. and Welch, E., 'The management of records', *Journal of the Society of Archivists*, **3**, 1968, 242-6.
4 Emmerson, P. (ed.), *How to manage your records: a guide to effective practice*, ICSA Publishing, Cambridge, 1989; Penn, I.A., Morddel, A., Pennix, G. and Smith, K., *Records management handbook*, Gower, 1989.
5 *Management of recorded information: converging disciplines*, Proceedings of the International Council on Archives' symposium on current records, National Archives of Canada, 15-17 May 1989, Durance, Cynthia J. (comp.), K.G. Saur, Munich etc., 1990.
6 Penn *et al.*, *op.cit.*, p. 3.
7 Cook, M., *Guidelines for curriculum development in records*

management and the administration of modern archives: a RAMP study, Unesco, General Information Programme and UNISIST (PGI-82/WS/16), Paris, 1982.

8 The term 'class' is defined in Chapter 3.

9 Cook, M., *The management of information from archives*, Gower, 1986, 48-9, illustrates an attempt.

10 This section was written with the example of the RM service of Pilkington Bros plc, St Helens, in view. Information from L. McDonald, the firm's records manager and archivist, 1991, and from Diana Stobbs, chair of the replacement servicing firm.

11 Dollar, C.M., *Electronic records management and archives in international organisations: a RAMP study with guidelines*, General Information Programme and UNISIST, Unesco, Paris, 1986, 77-8.

3

The arrangement of archival materials

This chapter describes what should happen when archival materials have been acquired by a repository, from the preliminary controls to the processes which follow. Arrangement and description are, with appraisal, the central professional work of archivists. Although the underlying principles upon which this work is based remain as stated by the classic writers,[1] there have been many important recent changes and developments. These apply to description rather more than to arrangement, but the two processes are closely linked.

The process of acquisition

The accessions register

When new material comes in to a repository, the first thing to be done is to record the facts of the transfer. The accessions register is the first component of a finding aid system. It is an essential element in such a system: acquisitions must always be recorded. This does not necessarily mean that the circumstances of the acquisition should always be directly communicated to the public. There is a strong case for making the facts of acquisition public as soon as possible, but at the same time it may be desirable to keep some of the information confidential, such as the name and address of the immediate source of the material, or the conditions of deposit. Decisions on these points should be made when the recording system is set up.

MAD2 provides a list of the data elements which are to be part of an accessions register. It suggests some alternatives as to how the register is to be seen in relation to the other parts of the finding aid system. The information in the accessions register can be seen as forming the last stage in the custodial history of a group (and hence open to the public as part of the finding aids), or as a private element in the repository's administrative files.

These alternatives are not mutually exclusive: one may use both. The chief point of difference is whether the information is regarded as being in the public domain or not. Clearly there are circumstances in which the conditions of immediate transfer to the repository are part of the necessary background, context and provenance information required for the interpretation of the data in the archive; and there are circumstances in which this information is not required by users.

Several repositories have published patterns for the layout and content of an accessions register. It should be easy for one of these, or for a synthesis of them, to be adopted as a national or international standard, on the lines of the following:

Repository:	
Accession number:	Reference code:
Date:	Bulk:
Provenance: Immediate source: Description:	
Conditions:	

Source: Merseyside Archives Liaison Group

Figure 3.1 An accessions register

Local and specialist networks

Accessions information forms the first part not only of an internal finding aid system but also of a system for data exchange between repositories with an affinity. This affinity may be territorial as in a regional network, or it may be subject-based; or, of course, both.

Some repositories have the custom of expanding their accessions register so that it can contain a summary description of the group. This can then be used immediately as a public finding aid, and the difficulties caused by description backlogs can then be avoided.[2]

There seems no reason why expanded accessions registers should not be included in cooperative networks, although of course there would have to be compatibility of standards between participants. As a general principle, it is better to complete full descriptions of archives before releasing them to the public, but everyone must admit that there are practical difficulties, and that backlogs are inconvenient. Shifting priorities to the early completion of summary descriptions may be a good option for an archives service.

Accessions data exchange in a network also raises the question of confidentiality. Generally, one may assume that agreements for data exchange should also provide for making the network (or some of the data on it) confidential. If this is done, a model system might assume that the full data available in the accessions registers of member repositories will be included centrally, so that the information is available to all the participating repositories (but not, in this context, to their users). Collaborative or networked accessions registers need a clear determination on terminology.

Joint or networked accessions registers obviously point the way towards a national information system. No doubt this will develop.

There is a difference between such a system and an online database like the ones familiar in North America. The latter are examples of cooperative bibliographic databases. The entries on them have been composed from data distilled from the repository's finding aids, in accordance with a strongly defined data standard. These databases are therefore final products; they are the result of completed work on archival accumulations. The same is true of the databases holding edited texts on the network JANET, although these are full-text, and not bibliographic. By contrast, accessions registers are the first, uncompleted step towards making the finding aids. They are primarily for management and control.

Central registration and enforcement of standards

The Royal Commission on Historical Manuscripts (HMC) was set up in 1869 to supplement in the private sector the arrangements then recently made for government records. It has the duty of getting knowledge about and seeking to protect archives and manuscripts held by owners outside the central government system. The work of the Commission is done by agreement and consent.

The National Register of Archives was set up in 1945 by the HMC, which at that time was actively engaged in promoting the foundation of county record offices. It receives reports and lists of archives which come to light or are received by repositories of all kinds, and maintains an access facility to these reports. Since its beginning the NRA has maintained an active programme of publishing finding aids to its holdings of lists, and the main development of recent years is the creation of a computer-based indexing system.

The HMC always reports upon cases in which its advice has been sought on choosing the most appropriate home for particular archives. This function implies that a national policy on determining acquisition policies could be developed.

The role of a central register in the establishment of a national system of collecting fields is clearly crucial. Such a system should recognize and safeguard the legitimate concerns of both territorial and specialist repositories, within the general context of the national interest.

A national register of archives should form part of every country's information system, the more so as such a register need not involve a major investment in staff or accommodation.

Controlling accession through repository management

Registering an accession is the first step in controlling a group through the various processes carried out in the repository. The data written into it can be linked later with the data in other description areas and sub-areas in the management information sector.[3]

In a computerized system, data can be put into a diary entry, so that the date and time of next action, including target date/times for the accomplishment of tasks can come up automatically on the diary schedules. A similar facility exists for repositories using the Archives and Records Control (ARC) segment in the RLIN database. The idea

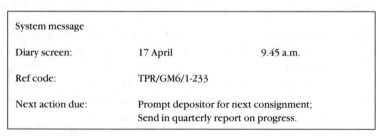

System message		
Diary screen:	17 April	9.45 a.m.
Ref code:	TPR/GM6/1-233	
Next action due:	Prompt depositor for next consignment; Send in quarterly report on progress.	

Figure 3.2 Example of a diary screen

of handling these management tasks through cooperative action is already established, however foreign it might seem in some repositories.

Continuing the process: arrangement and description

After registration, arrangement can begin.

Arrangement and description are closely linked but quite separate activities. Experience shows that they should continue to be distinguished: arrangement should come first, and should be completed; description can then be started. The activities which together we call arrangement are themselves separable into two. *Arrangement* – the broader term – is essentially an intellectual exercise, but *sorting* is the concrete activity which precedes and accompanies it.

Sorting is the activity of physically moving the components of an archival entity, to place them in order, in relation to the other components of the archive. During sorting, archivists gather and record information about the origin, make-up, use and content of the entity they are working on. The materials of the archive are themselves the main source of information in this process, and by their appearance and marking they offer the principal guidance to the best final arrangement. After gathering all the information available on the nature and history of the archive, archivists may go on to consult other, external, sources to confirm and complete the picture they have built up while handling the materials. To use cataloguing jargon, the materials themselves are said to be the chief source of information in preparing a description.

Arrangement is a process in which archivists seek to understand and record the original system or systems under which archives were created, and the order and sequence given by these to the components of the archive. The aim is to preserve and make clear the meaning of the original system and order. When arrangement is complete, both the method of storage given by the repository to the materials, and the way in which the descriptions are set out, will demonstrate this meaning.

Processing archival acquisitions should if possible be definitive. Brief or preliminary sorting and listing has often been a method used by hard-pressed archives services, as a way of avoiding the accumulation of backlog work. (Summary description can be associated with the accessions register, as mentioned above.)

Traditional wisdom is that the practice should not be regarded (in principle) as satisfactory or efficient, except as an emergency measure. The aim of archival processing is to bring the material fully under control and into use; in the language which has become standard in professional circles, archivists seek to establish both administrative and intellectual control over it. This means creating a set of finding aids that will let any part of the archive be found without trouble, and explain the nature and structure of the archive, so that any user's interest can be realized, and the potential value of the material exploited.

The creation of finding aids like this is one of the central duties of archivists and the source of one of the main pleasures of working with archives. The task demands an immersion in the subjects connected with the work of the creating agency, and it also demands an input of resources. There should be space to examine and arrange the materials, and time to analyse them. Other desirable resources might be access to reference facilities, the time to research and write, check and rewrite, and generally to consider the qualities and potential of the documents. Arranging and describing archives is academic work, and should conform to academic standards.

Most archival accumulations contain both information and items that are not familiar to the majority of users. The work of arranging and describing the materials necessarily makes the archivists who do it into experts: they are the ones who really know what is in the archive and what its significance is. They might not always have had proper time to research the background and get to know the full range of public knowledge in relevant fields. Many repositories lack convenient access to reference sources and related literature. It is often difficult, too, to devote the time needed to consult these freely. But the archivists who have worked on a particular group are the people who know best about it. To be one of these is to share one of the principal rewards of this work.

Arrangement should be definitive, but also rapid. Traditionally, a long delay between acceptance of the new accession and completion of the finding aids has often been regarded as regrettable but easily excusable. Getting the group into the repository assured its preservation. Full exploitation could wait, and therefore might tend to be postponed when there were more urgent claims on staff time. Delays were particularly likely when the group was very large.

Today such postponements are much less easy to defend. It is more apparent to us than to our predecessors that the commitment of public (or, at any rate, of dedicated) funds has to be justified by results. Management techniques can be used to cut intermediate processing, and arrange things so that priorities can be set and observed. Delays still occur, no doubt, but it is a professional concern that they should be controlled and reduced.

The processing of a group of archives should be managed as an integrated set of activities. It should be planned as a unitary project, the direct responsibility of one archivist (who may of course lead a team); it should have a degree of priority allocated to it, and a timetable within the work programme of the service. Deadlines for completion of the various stages of the process ought to be set and observed, but they should be deadlines which allow a sufficient degree of research and analysis. Those working on the arrangement and description of a group should have the opportunity to share in the making of these decisions and should have a clear idea of the objectives and timetable of their operation, its place in the overall work of the service, and when and how they should report their progress.

The theory of archival arrangement: moral defence

Arrangement is essentially an analytical process. It is intellectual, rather than physical. As Schellenberg said:

> Basic to practically all activities of the archivist is his analysis of records. This analysis involves him in studies of the organisational and functional origins of records to obtain information on their provenance, subject, content and interrelations .... Analytical activities are the essence of an archivist's work; the other activities that are based on them are largely of a physical nature.[4]

The work involved in archival arrangement therefore includes three elements:

- the physical operations of sorting the material
- the intellectual operations of analysis
- the management operations of determining levels and disposing of the materials for future action.

61

The two rules of procedure under which arrangement is carried out are:

1 Provenance: the archives of each originating agency should be kept together and managed as a unit.
2 Original order: within each unit of provenance, materials should be arranged in accordance with the order determined by the originating agency, or by subsequent administrations in which they were used as current records.

These rules, *mutatis mutandis*, are also applicable to the papers of a private person or family. The provenance of such papers is the person or family that created or assembled them originally. The original order is that set up by the person or family, or by subsequent persons or members of the family who were using the papers for their original purpose. (A practical problem is that there is often no evidence that there was a formal arrangement for these papers.)

Provenance

Archival entities should be managed as part of the archives of the agency or person that created them, and should not be confused with materials from another source. The archival product of a distinct organization or of the work of a prominent individual or family is termed a group (internationally 'fonds'). The term 'collection' which, following library practice, has often been used to mean an archive accumulation from a single provenance in the past, is usually inappropriate and is discouraged in national and international practice. ('Collection' is the appropriate term when a set of totally unconnected materials has been consciously brought together.)

Materials on similar subjects or of similar kinds may be found in archives from different origins. These should not be collected together but should be managed in their own groups, each group having its own provenance. A group need not be large, to be accepted as such; nor is there a limit to the number of groups held by a repository.

It is permissible for repositories to link together, conceptually, materials which are of related types or which deal with related subjects, but this collation remains conceptual and not physical. It is essentially a practice of repository management, and not a principle used in the arrangement of the materials themselves. For example, groups with a common characteristic may be brought together, conceptually, in management groups: this is discussed below, when levels of arrangement are defined.

A second example is where descriptions of groups, classes or items with common characteristics are assembled in a specialized finding aid. There should be a clear link between a finding aid like this and the main finding aid system, and users should be able to see what the background, context and provenance of any of the contents were. Several of the PRO Handbooks are examples of this type of collection.[5]

Groups often do not arrive in the repository in one consignment. If the accession which needs to be processed is not a complete group, its processing should be planned in association with the processing of the group as a whole. The accession may be of one or more classes, or it may be the latest consignment in the periodical transfer of a mixture of materials, including parts of a class previously received. There is no general rule for dealing with this situation. The choice is between (a) dealing with the new accession as a (partial) entity, and linking the finding aids, and (b) integrating the new accession into the old. Either way, the operation should be planned, and the principle of original order should be observed as far as possible.

A proper observance of the principle of provenance implies that archivists will assemble all the information on the background and origin of the entity which is needed to explain how it came to be, and how successive administrations have used it. The descriptions which eventually follow will include this information in an administrative and custodial history. The necessary data are acquired during the process of arrangement, and the research associated with it.

Provenance information should be included with the eventual finding aids, because it provides essential access points. Users may search for names or subject terms which occur in descriptions of provenance as a means of identifying groups relevant to their work. It is possible that this approach to searches of archival material is more important than approaches based on subject searches of descriptions of the content (although this is disputed).[6]

Original order

Within the entity, materials should be arranged in such a way as to record and demonstrate the order and system under which they were originally created and used. Physically, the materials should be sorted into appropriate levels of arrangement, as described below. The most appropriate order and system should become clear during the process of sorting.

Two problems are commonly met with in sorting:

    (a) where there are traces of a sequence of different arrangements resulting from administrative changes;

    (b) where it does not seem possible to discern any original order or system at all, or no consistent order.

The immediate provenance of a set of archives is often not the same as its original creation and use. Where these two are different, there is a need to know about both, as well as important changes which occurred in between. In description, these changes can be recorded in the administrative and custodial history area.

The immediate provenance is recorded in the accessions register, as it was known at the time of transfer to the archives service. Earlier administrative and custodial history is often discovered by archivists as they analyse the material.

Jenkinson thought that normal practice should be to treat the archive as it was during its latest period of administrative use, 'with the last Administration in which it played an active part'.[7] This no doubt is the most practical way. Any earlier system which had been superseded should be recorded. Usage over the years has endorsed Jenkinson's view.

However, common sense should always override the unthinking application of a rule. There are cases where the earliest, or earlier, system should, for compelling practical reasons, be restored at the expense of later ones. The later internal history of the group would then be recorded in description.

An example is provided by the German archives, part of the holdings of the National Archives of Tanzania. The German colonial administration up to 1917 established the original system. After the British conquest of the territory, the new administration disposed of the German files in new ways. Some were incorporated into the records of new or successor departments, and others were relegated to a closed store. Eventually, the German files were transferred to the archives, and it was then thought desirable to re-establish the original (German) system, and to record later developments, rather than do it the other way round. The specialized nature of the materials, and their language, made it necessary to manage the German archives in a separate subdepartment under control of a specialist. To preserve the later order of the materials would have resulted in their being dispersed through the archives of several departments. This would not have been convenient for any category of users and would not necessarily have provided an adequate moral defence.

The second case of difficulty, where there is no discernible original order, is discussed later in this chapter when dealing with arbitrary or conventional systems of arrangement.

Moral defence

A brief examination of the content of any archival entity can demonstrate the reason for these two rules of arrangement. Information on context and background is always necessary in order to interpret the information in an archival (or any primary) source. For example, a single letter cannot be understood without some knowledge of the continuing business of which it formed part. The letter is from a sender, to a recipient, and forms part of a sequence of events. The significance of the content of the letter cannot be understood until all these three variables are identified. The text of the letter may comment on various subjects, and give apparently intelligible information; but such comments must be interpreted in the light of ongoing interchanges between the correspondents, and in the light of the functional or administrative position occupied by each and their immediate purposes.

Individual letters are commonly held together in sequence, within folders ('files'). Files provide context and background for the letters considered as pieces, but the files themselves also require context and background. A file is part of an information storage system, which may be highly organized or very informal, but which in either case forms part of a larger system. To understand the whole activity recorded by the documents in a file one would have to know something about the system of which the file was a part. In particular, it would be necessary to know something of the administrative history of the creating agency: the names and offices of persons mentioned in the papers, the functions they exercised at different times, and so on. It might also be necessary to know something of the custodial history of the material, including the route by which it came into the hands of the repository.

At a higher level again, the meaning of correspondence or other records within a group can only be assessed when there is knowledge of the origin, purposes and development of the organization which created it.

These observations have been made with the model of an institutional archive in mind. They are still true if we think of a much more personal and much less strongly organized archive. The personal papers of an individual frequently demonstrate the same features. It is clear that single letters can only be interpreted if the reader knows who the sender and the recipient were. It is easy to see that in many cases this interpretation could be seriously affected also by a knowledge of the whole sequence of communication between these persons and others, by the offices or functional positions held by them, and by the external events which were occurring around them.

Provenance and context therefore provide information without which the individual items within an archive cannot be understood, or without which the significance of the information in them cannot be assessed. In addition, the sequence and method which was followed in the original creation can itself be used to provide additional information. It can reveal something of the policy-making procedures in a creating agency, and perhaps the movements or concurrent activities of the protagonists.

Because of this, information on their context, provenance and background is essential to the use and interpretation of archival documents. It must be compiled or preserved and made transparent to the user. Users are often not grateful for this service. They frequently prefer to concentrate upon the individual items whose information, they think, directly concerns them, without bothering too much about background, or the relationship of one archive to another. For many immediate purposes of reference, the confidence of these users is not too far misplaced; although it might be pointed out that a user who refers to a single archival item is often making use, unconsciously, of expert knowledge held in the background. For example, someone who looks up a name in a parish register is using expert knowledge already gained about the nature of a parish register and the entries in it.

The term 'metadata' has gained currency in recent years.[8] Coined as a term needed to describe system information required for the management of machine-readable archives, it seems now to have a wider use. Metadata are data which are essential to the understanding of a set of archives, but which are not actually derived from the archives themselves. They are data about the archives as materials, and directly descriptive of their system but not of their contents.

It appears then, that it is an important professional duty of archivists, central to their main mission, to take measures to compile and present the metadata that belong to an archive. They should display them in the finding aids and through the general organization of the materials in the repository. They concern, and are of benefit to, even those users who are not directly conscious of them.

The knowledge of context, provenance and background which is gathered by archivists during their work of arrangement, and set out by them in description, is their principal contribution to research and to public information systems, and sometimes it is the substance of their personal research. All these principles and activities together amount to what Sir Hilary Jenkinson, in a powerful and illuminating phrase, termed 'the moral defence of archives'.[9]

The theory of archival arrangement: levels

Archives are managed and described in hierarchically related levels. Archivists may choose and operate as many of these levels as seem appropriate in any case. Because of this, it has sometimes appeared that there is an infinitely extensible continuum of levels. In fact, experiments have shown that there are six such levels which can be fixed by empirically observable criteria. Any number of additional levels may be inserted between them, but the point at which any of the basic levels of arrangement is fixed remains constant in relation to the world of external phenomena.

The full list of determinable levels of arrangement is as follows:

Level no.	
0	Repository holdings
1	Management groups
2	Groups
3	Classes
4	Items
5	Pieces

The meaning of these levels is explained in the following sections.

When an accumulation of archives is analysed, it will usually be found that it divides naturally into levels of arrangement. This statement is made confidently even though it is admitted that each archive presents different characteristics, and that sometimes difficult decisions are needed.

The basic levels of archival arrangement have been recognized by all writers (British, American and others) since Jenkinson,[10] although MAD2 has recently introduced modifications. Another innovation brought in by MAD2 is the numbering of levels. In this system, the principal levels of arrangement are numbered by integers 1-5, and subsidiary levels between these, if required, may use decimal fractions of the leading integer. Any number of levels or subsidiary levels are allowed, and levels which are not useful in any particular case may be omitted.

These level numbers are intended only to help analysis and possible later data exchange. They should not be incorporated into public finding aids or reference codes, as this might tend to confuse inexpert users.

Levels based on physical realities: groups, classes, items

Three levels of arrangement are based directly on observable physical entities in the materials. They are summarized as follows:
Level 2: group (internationally, 'fonds'): this is the whole accumulation of archival material which arises from the work of some distinct organization or activity, or of a prominent individual. In many repositories, the group is treated as the main unit for both administrative and intellectual control. It is essentially a collectivity: a mass of materials brought into existence by a coherent and organized set of activities, with comprehensible relationships between its parts; but the definition does not make any requirement as to size. Most groups are large, but they need not be.
Level 2.xx: subgroups contain the archives of functional or administrative subdivisions of the organization which produced the group. Subgroups may be treated as separate units of administrative control, but in intellectual control can only be interpreted by reference to the group of which they are part.
Level 3: class (internationally, 'series'): these are the sets of materials which belong together because they have a physical

unity and a definable function in the administrative system which created the archive. In some repositories (mainly the very large ones) these are preferred as the basic units for both administrative and intellectual control. Classes are components of their group, but have a clear character of their own, which is linked to a specific recording role. In Australian practice, there is a standardized form for a register of series.

Level 4: item: this is the physical unit of handling, the actual object which can be picked up, packed for storage, and produced for use in the reading room. Items often contain sets of individual *pieces* (level 5), which are the smallest indivisible units of archival material, individual documents.

These three most fundamental levels of arrangement (group, class, item) are determined by external and objective criteria. They should not generally be the outcome of private judgement or arbitrary decisions. 'Group' is the name given to the archival product of a distinct organization, work or person. Classes have a recognizable physical character and can usually be identified by this. Items are physical unities. Archival arrangement can only be done by people who can recognize these levels of arrangement.

Not all levels of arrangement need be present in any particular set of archives, but it is believed that the characteristics of these basic levels can be observed in the archival materials of all countries and all circumstances; although in the case of any particular archival entity one or more of the levels of arrangement may be absent.

Level 2: Archives of the Am River Authority.
    Level 2.5: Finance and Audit
        Personnel Office

Level 3: Water Bailiffs' registers of occurrences.

Level 4: File of correspondence on riparian owners' claims, 1924–1936.

Level 5: Letter from Lord Fellowbrother, establishing claim, 12 June 1930.

Figure 3.3 Examples of the three fundamental levels

Levels based on management needs: management groups

The three physical levels of arrangement described above are the

Level			
1	Official & Public Records		
1.25	County Council		
1.5		Quarter Sessions	
		Lieutenancy & Militia	
		County Courts	
		Petty Sessions	
1.75			Northern Districts
			Southern Districts
1.25	Coroners		
	Schools		
1.5		Private Schools	
		Council Schools	
1.25	Boards of Guardians		
1.5	Turnpike Trusts		
	Local Authorities		
1.5		Boroughs	
		Urban Districts	
		Rural Districts	
		Civil Parish and Township	
1.25	Burial Authorities		
	Health Authorities		
1.5		Area Health Authorities	
		Hospitals	
1.25	Wills and Probate records		
1	Ecclesiastical archives		
1.25	Church of England		
1.5		Diocese	
		Dean and Chapter	
		Church Commissioners	
		Rural Deaneries	
		Ecclesiastical Parishes	
1.25	Methodists		
1.5	United Reformed Church		
	Baptists		
	Unitarians		
	Society of Friends		
1	Private archives		
1.25	Estate and Family		
	Solicitors, Estate Agents and Land Surveyors		
	Businesses		
1.5		Agriculture	
1.75			Agricultural supply firms
1.5		Banks and Building Societies	
		Chemical Manufacturers	
1.25	Antiquarian Collections		
	Societies and Voluntary Organizations		

Source: Cheshire Record Office Guide

Figure 3.4 A scheme of management groups and subgroups

70

ones used in arranging (and physically sorting) archival materials within a repository. In general practice they form part of a continuum of levels, which may be termed levels of archival management. Level 1 and its decimal fractions are reserved for a possible hierarchical series of such levels. It is customary (but not universal) for archivists to divide the holdings of their repository into conceptual (or management) groups. For example, it is quite usual for a local archives service to divide its holdings into management groups of cognate holdings. These may have labels such as 'official archives', 'private archives', 'ecclesiastical archives', and so on, on the model of a thesaurus. Often, the list of management groups is lengthy and elaborate, moving down from very broad to relatively narrow categories. Figure 3.4 gives an example of this.

The examples in this list are arranged in four levels of subordination. Broader and more general groupings are broken down into smaller and more specific ones. It would be possible to insert further management levels on the same principle.

The next level below, the group, must be established on the ground that there actually exists an accumulation of archives representing it. Neither ease of management nor the convenience of the user are the basis of groupings at or below level 2.

On the other hand, there is no compulsion to use the management level procedure at all. The essential point is that by passing from level 1 (or its decimal fractions) to level 2 (or its decimal fractions) one is passing from an arbitrary or conceptual grouping to an arrangement based upon physical facts. Level 2 (group) materials are actual archive accumulations which have been produced by distinct source organizations.

The main value of the management levels is that:

(a) they assist the archivists to achieve intellectual control of repository holdings. These groupings are based on an analysis of the repository's field of action. They provide a structure which can be used to inform survey work, and to indicate gaps in the information coverage of the materials held;

(b) the analysis of subjects, presented in a repository guide helps users to understand the range of information available, and the relationship of one group to another. It is a way of pointing out the value of provenance information, and making it comprehensible.

The level number '0' is allocated to the repository itself. A full description of any archival entity must, of course, contain a reference to the place where it is held, even though in particular contexts this information can be assumed. National or international schemes for data exchange must necessarily provide for repository identifications.

Defining groups

'Group' is a technical term which means the whole ensemble of archives produced by an organization which has a certain autonomy, or which could be recognized by an external observer as an entity in itself. By extension, the term is also used to mean the whole archive of a person, or of a set of persons who had any kind of independent collective character. This definition does not conflict with that of Jenkinson, who said that an 'Archive Group' (the term current then) consisted of 'the Archives resulting from the work of an Administration which was an organic whole, complete in itself, capable of dealing independently, without any added or external authority, with every side of any business which could normally be presented to it'.[11]

In a footnote, Jenkinson pointed out that this definition did not specify that the organization had to be of any particular size. In fact, groups can vary enormously in bulk. They can arise from big or small organizations (down to organizations run by single individuals); they can be big or small because of the character of the organization or because not many records have survived from it.

The international term which corresponds to 'group' is 'fonds', a French word successfully adopted into English. Using this international term has the advantage that it recalls the old, central principle of archive arrangement, that of 'respect des fonds':[12] the principle of provenance. Where a personal or corporate collector has brought together items from different sources, the resulting accumulation may be treated as a group, but the traditional term 'collection' may be more suitable. As interpreted today, the principle of provenance means (a) that materials from different provenances should not be mixed up together; and (b) that archivists must somewhere provide their clients with an explanation of the background, context and origin of any materials held.

A group is essentially an aggregate, and the term does not say anything about the internal arrangement of that aggregate. Levels below group refer to smaller, component, aggregates. Subgroups or classes can be considered in two ways. They are units which form part of a larger archive, and they are entities in themselves, containing smaller components. This is also true of items, which are entities within a group (and usually also within subgroup and/or class), but which may also themselves contain smaller components, pieces. Pieces are the irreducible minimum components, single documents, but since these are not usually the units of handling, they are not necessarily considered when arrangement is being discussed.

Any archival entity - an actually existing body of material - must necessarily belong as a whole to one of these levels. However, archivists need only use those levels which are actually present in the materials they are arranging. Thus it is perfectly possible to have a group which contains no subgroups or classes.[13] Against this, it is hard to imagine a situation where the group level is absent, since by definition any archival entity must have a provenance: it must have been created by a person or organization whose work it then represents. A group is the totality of archives which were produced by (or which have survived from) a distinct or autonomous creating agency.

Although the definition seems clear at first sight, there are often difficulties in establishing what exactly should be recognized as a group. Many organizations are easily recognizable as autonomous in the sense intended by the definition. The archive of a landed estate or family; of a small manufacturing firm; of a country solicitor's office; of a research chemist - no archivist would feel much difficulty in accepting the whole accumulation of records from any of these as a group. But what about the archives of a department of a county council, or the division of a ministry? When managing the archives of the Methodist Church, do we take all the churches in a circuit to be the group, or the archives of an individual congregation? If a manufacturing firm is owned by an umbrella group, where should we set the group level? It is clear that there is a connection between the level at which the group is recognized, and wider aspects of the organization, as well as component parts.

The fact is, that most organizations and personal activities belong in a continuum of hierarchical levels of some sort. An hierarchical plan can be drawn, in which broader organizations contain within themselves sets of smaller participating organizations. They all belong to the same overall business or administrative structure, and each part may have a certain autonomy and also a certain dependence. A complicating factor is that in these complex relationships between bodies, there may be superseded or defunct components.

The nature of this kind of continuum can be illustrated very easily.

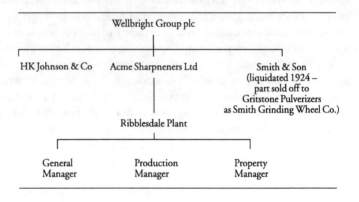

Figure 3.5 Relationships between organizations

In this example, the archives of Wellbright (the overall owner) would be regarded as those of a group (level 2). In practice, the archives of Acme should also be set at level 2. There might be a case for treating Ribblesdale, one of the geographically distinct plants owned by Acme, as a subgroup of that firm. If the Ribblesdale archives were at all substantial, however, it would be much better practice to set Ribblesdale also at level 2, and provide cross-references.

Smith & Son is an interesting case. There are several possibilities. Smith & Son might be regarded as a subgroup of Wellbright, or (for preference) as a group on its own. Again, Smith Grinding Wheel could be a subgroup of Gritstone, but it would probably be better placed as a group on its own. The determining factor is the whereabouts and nature of the actual archives. If the material actually produced by that administration is substantial in amount and is physically distinct from the records of the umbrella owner company, then the indicators are pointing to its treatment as a separate group. If on the other hand Smith & Son was always administered from the offices of Wellbright, and its records are not substantial or distinct, then the indicators are towards treatment as a subgroup.

74

To sum up: in defining what is a group, there is a clear guideline. The definition should follow the physical existence of an actual body of archives. If an organization has created a set of archives, and this accumulation of material is being accessioned by an archives service for management, then the probability is that this organization should be recognized as the creator of a group.

This guideline and definition stands irrespective of any relationship of dependency which the creating organization might have with any other. In the example above, any of the firms which produces an accumulation of archives of its own, may be treated as a group, no matter whether the firm appears in the first, second or third (or other) ranks of the table. (Of course, in the description, the nature of the dependency must be explained.) If there is an organisation which has any degree of independent personality - if it has a name and an address, for example - and if it produces an accumulation of archives in the course of its activities, then those archives should form a group. In the example, there is the possibility of five or more groups (one with three subgroups) merely in the wording shown. There is no limit to the number of groups which a repository can legitimately hold. Groups do not have to be big or small; they only have to have a distinct provenance.

This rule represents what has been the best practice in the past. Confusion has sometimes arisen because the hierarchical table of dependence in a chain of organizations looks rather like the conceptual table of activities, organizations and functions which appear in the table of management levels. It is important to see the difference, and not treat levels of dependence between organizations as equivalent to a kind of thesaurus of public activity.

An important reason for linking the group level closely to the identity of any organization which has had a coherent enough existence to allow it to produce an archive, is that there needs to be provision for managing that archive in the future. A body which produces an archive should be able to consult directly with the custodian and manager of that archive. If the chain of communication must lie through other bodies which have some relationship of control or dependence, then unnecessary difficulties are caused.

The argument is similar to that for giving classes a priority in the administration of large archives services. Where there is continuity of administrative practice, but great discontinuity in the management structures of the creating agency, then there is a case for making the class the fundamental level of arrangement. Records belonging to these will continue to accrue to existing classes, even though the line manager concerned is constantly being changed. These changes can be explained in background descriptions: users will want to have access to all the material in a class, whatever its nominal source. This practice is now well established as an alternative to control by group, and can be considered by any archives service that is in the situation described above.

Defining subgroups

As soon as sorting begins, it becomes clear whether or not there are natural subdivisions within a group. To distinguish them, analysis is necessary. Two different criteria may be used, and each kind results in a different level of arrangement. The group may be divided as follows into:

- subgroups
  and/or
- classes.

These are different from each other, and the distinction should be borne in mind.

Subgroups are the archives of internal divisions of the creating organization, or, if there are no clear structural divisions there, they are the archives of clearly definable functions. In the example in Figure 3.5, the three managerial departments are subgroups of Ribblesdale plant because none of them is an autonomous unit: the archives of the production manager can only be understood if read in conjunction with those of the general manager, and vice versa. A more complete analysis of the firm's structure could be used to show how further subgroups, and sub-subgroups, etc., can be distinguished within the total body of a group.

Individual persons can also originate groups. In these cases, if there are subgroups they will be based upon distinguishable functions in the individual's career. For example, if the originator was a member of a commission of inquiry, the papers arising from that activity might be a subgroup. Otherwise, subgroups might be discerned even if the function was not institutional: so family affairs might form one.

Typical titles of subgroups might be the following:
Office Management Services
Registrar's Department
Tyne Bridge consultancy
legal and court papers
railway link project.

The rule is, then, that subgroups should reflect the different structures and functions that may have existed in the creating organization, or different areas of activity undertaken by it. If no such divisions can be perceived, then it is best to omit this level.

Archivists sometimes set up schemes of arrangement which provide for 'standard' subgroups, reflecting the main functions of the organism: for example, policy and direction; finance; legal; property; personnel and production. This kind of analysis, on the model of a classification scheme, may be useful in providing a kind of check-list by which it can be seen whether all the valuable material has been received. It is particularly appealing when the archives of a number of similar organizations are being collected. It may also help users to see the pattern of information held.

Useful as this practice may be, it is important not to see the device as the equivalent of a classification scheme in a library. The existence or not of a particular function or the subgroup that would represent it, is something that should be determined by the facts of archival survival, not by the need to fill a predetermined category.

It is not necessarily the case that any given group may contain any subgroups at all. However, it is sometimes reasonable to set up subgroups based on the convenience of managing the group in smaller, more easily handled, portions. (The question of convenience groupings is discussed below.) A good guideline would be that if there are no natural subgroups, the best alternative would be to go down a level and use the classes instead; only if these are not helpful would it be desirable to create a convenience subgroup.

Defining classes

Classes are sets of archival materials which belong together because they are of like kind. They were created and used as a system, and one would normally expect that a class would have a collective name, by which it was called when the class was in current administrative use.

Typical class names are the following:
  purchase ledgers
  minutes of Management Committee
  Central Office filing system
  patent files
  'grey folders'.

If there were no classes in use in the original system or (which may be the same thing) if all the items in a group belonged to a single class, this level is best omitted.

The distinction between subgroups and classes is not always quite clear, in practice. The theory has been clear enough for many years, and it has been explained by several writers.[14] This has not prevented the two from being confused in daily practice. It is not difficult to find examples – the *Guide to the contents of the PRO* provides many.

Australian practice is to take classes (and not groups) as the basic level of archival management.[15] This innovation was accepted as a way of dealing with the notorious problems of administrative instability: when departmental structures were changed within an organization, the classes produced by particular corporate functions continued unchanged, but in a new context. By managing the class as a continuing entity, and linking the descriptions of departmental or functional changes, acceptable continuity was possible. In a government setting, this approach is practical and efficient. However, even here, confusion between subgroups and classes can be observed occasionally.

Archivists analysing groups, and sorting them into their component subgroups and classes, should remember that these collectivities are things that can be seen experientially. If they do not exist in the materials, then they should be omitted.

It is perfectly possible, and common, to have a group which has no subgroups. (Although many archives treated as subgroups would perhaps have been better dealt with as groups in their own right.) It would be less common, but still perfectly possible, to have a group with no classes. Some groups or subgroups might contain several classes, others only one class, others none; and so on. No level of archival arrangement is compulsory,[16] although group and item seem to be universal and unavoidable.

If classes are taken as the basic level for management of the service, the principle of provenance can be observed by linking the class descriptions to the relevant group descriptions, held in a different file.

When this method is adopted, the group descriptions are sometimes regarded as 'authority' files. This is because they are held in the background, and called up when a reference to them is needed; and because they can incorporate authoritative titles.

Arrangement within the group

Arrangement is preceded by and accompanies the physical process of sorting. Groups are normally complex. Arrangement includes the process of sorting the various components of the group and putting them into order relative to each other. In the sorting process there are three aims:

    (a) to recognize subdivisions in the whole mass which will help administrative control of it;

    (b) to ensure that information necessary to the interpretation of the archive is kept and made clear (the moral defence of it); and

    (c) to prepare the ground for description, and hence the intellectual control of the group.

In practical terms and at the beginning, the first of these aims is the most important. Most groups are large, or very large. If a group is small, arrangement is probably less complex, and can be done faster. To assist rapid progress, archivists should aim to break up unmanageable masses of material into portions of reasonable size. Wherever possible these portions should represent the natural subdivisions of the material, and fall into the standard levels of arrangement. There are cases where this is not possible, and here units of convenience may be considered.

Units of convenience

If there are no subgroups or classes, then subdivisions may be established which are more or less arbitrary. In these circumstances, conventional subgroups might be invented, to correspond with sets of papers concerned with related activities or functions. Alternatively, or as well, composite classes can be formed of papers with some common characteristic.

Item level can also be used as a management convenience. Single papers can be assembled into folders of like materials, which would then be used as units of handling.

It is always necessary that big groups should be divided out into units suitable for physical management and into units which can be described and retrieved. It is also useful to make sure that the units of handling are convenient for the various processes that are to be done on them, such as repair. These divisions of the main mass of material are established while sorting.

Internal structure and order

The overall aim in arrangement is to recognize and confirm (or restore) the original order of the records. Before sorting, archivists should note any evidence of original order or system which may be there, and particularly they should take care not to destroy original reference or finding codes or markings. They would not be likely to do this when the markings appear on documents, but writing on (perhaps dirty and torn) bundle wrappings is often vulnerable. Archivists should also record what was done during sorting if it is not obvious from the resulting analysis. If it is important enough, this can be summarized in the archivist's note sub-area of the eventual description.

Groups which have no internal structure are usually personal papers. In some cases, the originator never had a systematic arrangement. Other cases might be the records of primitive organizations where the records were not subdivided systematically during their period of currency.

If it is really necessary to provide an internal structure, there are three alternative methods which could be used:

> function
> physical form
> arbitrary orders: chronological
> > > alphabetic
> > > numeric

If one of these has to be chosen, choice should follow the order of priority shown in this table.

Arrangement by function probably at least approximates to arrangement by what might have been an original order. If there is a practical need for subdivision, those parts of the archive which illustrate a field of activity, an official or unofficial function of the originator, should be picked out and offered status as a subgroup, even though there may be no evidence that the originators them-

Level 2.5	*London Safety First Council*	
Level 3	2/1 Council meetings, minutes	1931-1940
	2/2 General Purposes Committee minutes	1917-1940

Source: Archives of the Royal Society for the Prevention of Accidents.

Figure 3.6 Example of arrangement by function

selves recognized such a distinction. If there is no need for subdivision, then the subgroup (or any other) level may be omitted.

Arrangement by form may also have a close relationship with a possible original system. This resembles arranging by class. The earliest administrations in the British Isles tended to follow this method. For example, in court records, it was customary, before quite modern times, to file like kinds of record with like kinds: writs with writs, affidavits with affidavits, etc. This system must have had disadvantages at the time, since it would never have been easy to examine all the records of a single case. On the other hand, retrieval of any one document would have been easy, and storage would have been economical because the documents would tend to have the same size and shape. These advantages might still be attractive.

However, arrangement by function is preferable to arrangement by form. For example, if there are many minute books, they should be arranged, if possible, under the names of the committees they served (arrangement by function), rather than as a general class in themselves (arrangement by form). Figure 3.6 shows an example of this.

Arbitrary orders form the third and lowest level of priority. This means that most often they are used within function or form groupings, to establish the order of items or pieces. The choice of one system or another often depends on the nature of the materials and the titles or references that are attached to them.

Chronological or alphabetical orders could be used in the case of loose correspondence, for example. Chronological orders must of course be based upon the dates of the original documents, but there are some difficulties here. For example, should the date of composition (recommended, if it can be established), of despatch, of receipt or of registration (if applicable) be preferred? There is no general rule. The most practical method should be adopted. It is important to be consistent and to explain the method used in the headnote or macro description.

Alphabetical orders, sorting on the name of the correspondent, could be chosen for sets of letters, as this might give some coherence to the story of a person's relationships, and as there is a natural data element (the correspondent's name) which can be used to sort on. Alphabetical order is not so easy where the data element is the title of an item. The keywords which occur in titles are not necessarily useful for this kind of purpose.

Level 4:	5/16 Extraordinary general meeting	17 May 1951
	24 Report on Service, Accounts & Subscriptions	
		1960

In this example of file titles, the alphabetical order is effective as a device for placing items in order down the page. It is not effective as a retrieval device, since the order is decided only by whatever term happens to come first, whether or not it is a term which describes the contents of the file.

Numerical (or alpha-numerical) sorting should only be adopted when there is an original numbering present, as there might be with registered papers, or a series of case records. Allocating a sequence of individual numbers to papers within a group (other than the reference code, which follows arrangement) is not recommended practice as it tends to dissolve natural collectivities.

Original means of access to the archives (for example, indexes) should be preserved and if possible kept in use as part of the final intellectual controls.

Sorting

In general, it is best to sort all the materials physically before any other work is done. If possible this should be done in a place where there is plenty of room to set out piles of material, where these will not be disturbed.

The optimum sequence of activities is as follows:

- sort the materials, noting natural subdivisions and sets
- proceed from larger units to smaller (subgroups first, then classes, then items)
- while doing this, compile information on the originating system, its changes and development (or degeneration) over time.

When the sort is complete, consolidate the arrangement by boxing and storing, and by writing identifying codes in pencil on the boxes. These can be changed to permanent reference codes (if necessary) when the description is done.

Location

Traditionally, sorted archival materials are stored in archival (or structural) order. This term, normal in professional practice, indicates the order which has been established by following the principles of provenance and original order. The order of the materials on the shelf would then follow the hierarchical and logical arrangement into which they have been sorted. This is still the normal practice in many repositories, and in general it is to be recommended. However, increasingly repositories find that this method of storage uses unnecessary amounts of shelf space. These repositories prefer to store the sorted materials by random access order, or by following some convenient principle such as shelving by size. There are two rules:

1 Archival (structural) order must be preserved and demonstrated in the finding aids, in such a way that any user can clearly understand what the original system and order was.
2 Each unit of location (normally either a box or an item) should have an address by which it can be identified and retrieved.

Reference codes

When the physical processes of arrangement have been completed, it may be useful to allocate reference codes to the materials. These codes can then be written on to the boxes or on to the originals themselves, in order to consolidate the arrangement and ensure that it is possible to locate any part of the archive.

Some thought should be given to the design of reference codes within the service. It is not easy to change them after the finding aids have been released, because users will have used them in citation. Computerization of the finding aid system may have an effect on the form of reference codes, and this should be taken into account. It is important to make a right choice of system.

The first function of a reference code is simply to allow the materials to be controlled. The coding of any particular item should

```
┌─────────────────────────────────────────────────────────────┐
│           Borsetshire Record Office DBT/CM1/16,p.6            │
│ Level 0 Repository name                                       │
│     Level 1 Deposited archives: D                             │
│         Level 1.5 Boroughs: B                                 │
│             Level 2 Tollmere Borough Council: T               │
│                 Level 2.5 Committee of Management: CM         │
│                     Level 3 Committee minutes: 1             │
│                         Level 4 Minute book no.: 16          │
│                             Level 5: page 6                   │
└─────────────────────────────────────────────────────────────┘
```

Figure 3.8 Example of a reference code

therefore be unique. It is helpful if the code also gives information on the provenance and relationships of the items to which it is attached.

This example shows a reasonably clear and simple reference code (it is rarely possible to have one much simpler than this). If there had been more levels of arrangement, it would not have been so transparent. There is a general recommendation that full reference codes should not attempt to demonstrate every level of arrangement if the result would be unattractive or difficult for users. In many cases, it is possible to include an element for each level, and it is recommended that this should be done wherever possible.

It is also recommended that levels down to subgroup should be represented by alphabetical characters, and levels for class and below should be represented by numbers. This practice follows the long tradition of the PRO, and can often be quite easily workable. In other cases, there are difficulties which result in the recommended usage being set aside.

At one time, it was conceivable that the alphabetical part of the reference code would be mnemonic. For example:

QSB   Quarter Sessions Books
DONT   Deposited papers: O'Neill of Tara

Nowadays there are too many groups and subgroups to allow this expansive practice. We must accept that reference codes are merely technical devices to allow controlled storage and retrieval.

Classification schemes

Classification was not listed as one of the sorting methods, as it is a technology of limited value to archivists. Classification is the process of arranging items under the rules of a predetermined scheme, usually an analysis of the universe of knowledge in a relevant field. This is useful in libraries, where the units of handling (books) are autonomous, and can be classified in any way that seems useful for storage and retrieval. Archives have to be arranged in accordance with their provenance and original order, and these are unique to each group.

There are circumstances in which purpose-designed classification schemes can be useful in archival management. These are the following:

1 To provide a structure for the arrangement of the archives of different institutions of like kind.
2 To provide a vocabulary and structure for the access points by which information is retrieved from the finding aid system in a repository.
3 To structure the finding aid system itself.

Up to the present, the second of these purposes has been the most useful. This is illustrated by the history of the subject indexing classification scheme which was issued by the NRA in 1969.[17] Although long since abandoned by the NRA, this scheme has continued in use in several repositories. It will no doubt continue to have a general usefulness until a revised scheme is issued.

Readers will have noticed that the scheme for setting our management levels, an example of which was given above in this chapter, is also a kind of classification scheme. There is potential value in developing analysis of subjects and institutions in this way, as a help to structuring aspects of archival management. As national and international cooperation develops, the need for authority lists such as this will increase.

Notes and references

1 Muller, S., Feith, J.A. and Fruin, R., *Manual for the arrangement and description of archives*, drawn up by direction of the Royal Netherlands Association of Archivists, 1898.
2 Cheshire Record Office system; information from Mr Jonathan Pepler, Principal Archivist.
3 References to descriptive practices, here and later, are couched in the technical language of MAD2. Technical terms are explained in this and the following chapter.

4 Schellenberg, T.R., *Modern archives: principles and techniques*, Chicago, 1956, 118.

5 For example, Alford, B.W.E. (ed.), *Economic planning 1943-51: a guide to documents in the Public Record Office*, PRO Handbooks no. 26, HMSO, 1992.

6 Lytle, R.H., 'Intellectual access to archives: provenance and content indexing methods of subject retrieval', *American archivist*, **43**, 1980, 64-75; **44**, 1981, 191-207. There has been further discussion of the point in later issues of this journal but no further systematic research.

7 Jenkinson, C.H., *A manual of archive administration*, 2nd ed. (revised), Lund Humphries, 1965, 104.

8 Promoted, and probably coined, by Charles Dollar. See, in particular, his paper 'The impact of information technologies on archival principles and practices', delivered at the archival seminar at the University of Macerata, 1990.

9 Jenkinson, *op.cit.*, 83.

10 *op.cit.*, 115-16; M.Baudot, 'Les instruments de recherche', in Ministère des Affaires Culturelles, Association des Archivistes Française, *Manuel d'archivistique*, Paris, 1970, 243-94; O.W. Holmes, 'Archival arrangement: five different operations at five different levels', *American archivist*, **27**, 1964, 21-41.

11 *op.cit.*, 101.

12 *Dictionary of archival terminology*, 1984, 130. Jenkinson used the phrase 'respect pour les fonds', which looks anglicized.

13 In the Federal Archives system of Germany, there are considered to be no classes, simply fonds and items. It might be argued that in that context, all items within a single group belong to a single class (viz. 'files'). However, in practice this simply means that level 3 can be ignored. This approach can be compared with the Australian practice, where the class is considered fundamental.

14 Although assumed by earlier writers, the distinction has been made quite clear by R.H. Lytle's PhD thesis, *Subject retrieval in archives: a comparison of the provenance and content indexing methods*, University of Maryland, 1979.

15 Based on developments from the work of P.J. Scott, 'The record group concept, a case for abandonment', *The American archivist*, **29**, 1966, 493-504. See also Healy, S., 'The classification of modern government records in England and Australia', *Journal of the Society of Archivists*, **11**, 1990, 21-6.

16 The international *Statement of principles concerning archival description* gives a diagram illustrating groups (fonds) with different components.

17 National Register of Archives *Subject index schema and word-list*, Royal Commission on Historical Manuscripts, 1969. This project was associated with Felicity Strong.

4

Archival description

General aims

The previous chapter describes how the analysis of a mass of archival materials is done during sorting and final arrangement. Description should not start until all that has been completed.

The aims of description are as follows:

(a) to assure that moral defence has been provided for the archive by recording and setting out the evidence of its origin and structure;

(b) to provide administrative control of the materials by identifying their components and their storage place;

(c) to provide intellectual control by enabling users to identify items and to exploit the materials in reference or research;

(d) to extend the means of exploitation to users outside the repository.

This statement is somewhat bald and should be supplemented by another, which was produced by the working party of the Society of American Archivists in 1989: 'Archival description is the process of capturing, collating, analysing, and organizing any information that serves to identify, manage, locate and interpret the holdings of archival institutions and explain the contexts and records systems from which those holdings were selected.'[1]

This second summary of the aims of description brings out some fundamental facts. First, it points out that description is an activity that completes every aspect of the work and management of an archives service. Second, and most important, it points out that archival description has to provide two kinds of information:

• information (metadata) about the circumstances of the origin and technical formatting of the material, the media used, its function in the original context, and its adventures since;

- information about the materials themselves: their physical shape and nature, and the information held within them.

Both kinds of information must be present (at least in some form) in every archival description.

Standards

This chapter has been written in the light of the rules for archival description which have been published since 1990. It pays particular attention to the rules currently accepted in Britain, which are laid down in versions of the *Manual of archival description* (MAD);[2] and to the international standard for archival description adopted by the International Council on Archives (ICA) in 1992.[3]

All description standards published so far assume that repositories will have a house standard which will extend and customize the general rules. No universal norm can be expected to be suitable in all respects for shaping the work which is done within the service. We should not be surprised, therefore, if the descriptive work of one repository does not look exactly the same as that of another. The general rules embody the fundamental principles of archive management, and it is hard to imagine a situation in which these principles could be successfully dispensed with.

The theory of the representation file

MAD2 sets out the theory of the representation file, for this underlies all archival description. By making clear what it is we are doing when we describe a document or a set of documents, it makes it possible to be clear about the immediate objectives, and to plan the shape and purpose of the descriptions which will result.

The theory of representation is that while original archives must necessarily be stored on the shelf in one set physical order and location (and usually in closed containers), representations of the originals can be multiplied and stored in any order and in any place that is considered useful.

Normally, the physical storage order will be the structural (or archival) order, established during arrangement. If this is so, the physical order records and demonstrates the system which was used to create and use the materials originally. MAD2 recommends that this structural order should normally be the order in which the materials are stored. This is because the moral defence of the archives is then established in the physical arrangement of the materials, and does not depend on users being able to interpret a finding aid.

However, if there are compelling reasons (for example, of repository management), it is possible to store archival materials in some other order (random, or ranged in sizes, or according to the chronology of accession), and to arrange the finding aids so that the structural order can be perceived and reconstructed on paper. The essentials are that the original arrangement is explained, and that any part of the archive can be identified and retrieved. In any case, since archival materials are normally stored in boxes or containers, which are kept in closed storage and are not open to browsing, it is inevitable that retrieval of any kind must depend on the use of a finding aid.

Finding aids are collections of descriptions, which represent the original materials for the purposes of management and control. A file of descriptions is a *representation file*. (The term 'representation file' is not intended to be used as a name for actual finding aids in daily life in a repository, but is simply a statement of their theoretical function.)

Since management has different needs at different times, representations should be shaped to accord with these needs. Hence the need for a rule that states that each representation must be designed for a specific purpose. The effectiveness of any one representation can be judged by its effectiveness in achieving the stated purpose.

This rule, like most of MAD2's rules, is very broadly stated. It simply means that there can be no universal model for making representations of originals. If what is needed, for example, is a location or shelf register (to assist with stock control), then the representation file only needs to contain data elements such as location code, reference code, and an indication of bulk, and perhaps physical description and

Shelf list	
Room 2, bay 16, shelf B	AA24/28-32 6 boxes

Figure 4.1 Example extract from a shelf list

condition, as demonstrated in Figure 4.1.

This entry in a representation file clearly contains only a minimum of information. At the other extreme one may imagine a set of representations which are aimed at giving users a good appreciation of the contents of the materials. The fullest form of this is where the representation file becomes a *surrogate* file: where the representation actually replaces the original for most purposes.

A *calendar* is a set of descriptions so complete that users can read them at a distance and find virtually all the primary information held by the originals. Calendars normally contain all the specific information held in the text of an original, but omit the phrases of common form, and do not use the original wording (except for occasional quotations). Full-text transcripts naturally have the same characteristic of presenting all the content information. Even in these cases, of course, surrogation is never quite total. There will always be a small group of users who need to see the original, whose enquiry will be based upon the physical nature of the carrier (parchment, paper), the ink, extraneous markings or some other point of diplomatic.

In the days of Jenkinson, it was expected that most descriptive work would consist of editing or transcribing original texts, in order to make the content of these available outside the repository. Only reluctantly did this writer admit the necessity for giving time to making finding aids which did not allow for surrogation.[4]

Most finding aids lie between the extremes of the calendar and the shelf list, and one of the reasons for this is that their purpose is less clearly defined. Most of the finding aids encountered by users in the reading room contain some data on the following:

- background, context and provenance;
- the physical nature and condition of the materials;
- the information contained in them (generally there is perceptible emphasis on the last).

These finding aids will be used by readers to identify originals they wish to consult, and they will also be used by the staff to help them in managing the holdings of the repository. General-purpose finding aids are therefore almost standard in most repositories. It is possible that more attention should be given to the specific purpose of a finding aid before it is made, and that finding aids systems should be more complex than has been customary in the past.

Different representations may of course be made of the same set of originals. These different representations may be arranged in different ways. There are no rules about this: imagination and inventiveness should be given free play. There are some basic rules about finding aids, however, which are as follows:

1 The main representation file should be set out in structural (or archival) order so that it can record and explain the system which first created the archives, and so provide moral defence.
2 The other representation files can be set out selectively in alternative ways.
3 The finding aids as a whole should be treated as a system. This should have cross-references, linking features and consciously designed access points.
4 There should be provision for authority files which will control the public interface with the finding aids system.

Finding aids systems

The term 'finding aid' does not have a technical definition. It simply means something that helps users to identify archival materials. There are all sorts of finding aids. A description, on the other hand, must definitely be a representation of some set of original materials, which has been constructed for a particular purpose. Finding aids always include (and are often entirely composed of) some descriptions; or sets of descriptions are combined to form a finding aid. Finding aids are the one vital tool of archive management.

The term 'finding aid' highlights one essential feature of archival descriptions – their use in tracking complex lines of enquiry. Because these lines are complex, often obliging users to investigate more than one group and frequently more than one repository, the way one finding aid is related to others is important.

The relationship is between the different representations of one set of originals, and the finding aids which refer to different sets of originals. Readers may need to see different finding aids which relate to one group, or they may need to look at the finding aids which relate to several groups (or several repositories) – or both.

Hence it is clear that it is the business of a repository to construct finding aids systems: that is, organized and planned sets of representations with links between them. The component parts of a system should act together, and should be easy for the average user to comprehend.

Finding aids systems should contain:

- a principal representation file
  (in structural order)
- secondary representation files
  (in subject or other orders)
- retrieval aids
  (indexes, guides).

Finding aids systems also contain different combinations of descriptions. For example, a combination might be termed 'vertical' (although this term is not used in MAD2), when it includes descriptions of one related set of materials at different levels of arrangement.

Group description	)	
Subgroups	)	of the same group
Classes	)	
Items	)	
Index		

(This particular set can be called a *catalogue*.)

Figure 4.2 Vertical sets of finding aids

Alternatively, or as well, a finding aids system can contain a horizontal assembly of descriptions, all at the same level of description but referring to different archival holdings.

Horizontal sets of finding aids may include:

- A guide containing management group and group descriptions (perhaps also subgroups arranged with their groups) of all holdings in a repository.
- A catalogue containing a sequence of descriptions of a group and its components, in order, with an index.

Levels of arrangement as applied to descriptions

Levels of arrangement have to be used in the structure of finding aids. There is a direct correspondence: if a group is being used for management purposes, there should be a corresponding group description in the finding aids system. Recognizing a class leads to writing a class description, and so on. Each of these levels is likely to demand special characteristics in the descriptions applied to them. Models are given later in this chapter.

It is a general principle that description should proceed from the larger aggregates to the smaller. In this context, the classical model is the description of a group (fonds: level 2). Where there is no strong reason against it, it would be best to complete the description of the whole group before embarking on bits of it, the subgroups (if any), the classes (if any) and in the end, the items.

The multi-level rule

One of the clearest of all the rules of description is the multi-level rule. This states that all archival description should be done at two or more levels. MAD2 goes on to explain how these levels relate to each other, and from this analysis it becomes plain (although this is not stated explicitly anywhere in MAD2) that a second characteristic of descriptive levels exists, distinct from the levels of arrangement.

This characteristic is indicated by the special labels which MAD2 gives to linked descriptions in a multi-level finding aid. They are termed 'macro' and 'micro' descriptions. The relationship between these is not directly connected with the levels of arrangement: it is not absolute, as are levels of arrangement, but relative, as between two or more descriptions.

To illustrate this, an extreme case may be taken. Suppose that it is desired to write a description of a group which consists of only one document. Such a situation might well exist, although it would be rare: imagine the case of a politically active family whose archive has been destroyed by an accidental fire except for one document which

level 2	XY	Bagwith papers	1662
		The archive of Thomas Bagwith and his son William Bagwith, successively Keepers of the Petty Seal, 1660-72 and 1672-80, was kept at Bagwith Hall until the fire of 1948 in which all was destroyed except the following item, which was deposited in Felpersham University Library in February 1946.	
level 4	XY/1	Letter of Charles II to Thomas Bagwith, [?] Oct. 1662	
		Contains details of the king's itinerary.	
		2 pages, stained by damp.	
		Holograph signature.	

Figure 4.3 Example of macro and micro descriptions

94

was on loan to an archive repository. This document needs to be described so that it can be managed and used. The description should be multi-level, so that it will be described both as a group, and as an item. The result will look like Figure 4.3.

In the example in Figure 4.3, the level 2 description is the macro description, and it governs the level 4 description, which is the micro description. Levels 2 and 4 are absolutes, determined by the nature of the material (level 2: the archive of a distinct organization or entity; level 4: the unit of physical handling). Using these as macro and micro depends on the context and the design of the finding aid.

This example shows the different characteristics of the two levels and their relationship. The macro description deals with the material from the point of view of generalities, and gives its background, context and provenance. Macro descriptions can also summarize the whole aggregate which is being described. The micro description deals with details proper to the item as object (and of course in more normal groups will deal with such details case by case).

The macro description is also used (if appropriate) to give common information: that is, data which occur in, or apply to, all or most of the entities described in the following micro descriptions. This convention avoids the need to repeat data elements in a series of entries, occurring time after time.

The multi-level rule is no more absolute than any other rule or practice in archive administration. Each archive presents different problems; each finding aid presents special features. Consequently it is possible to find archival descriptions which exist only at one level. Where this is so, it is the macro description which must be present: the moral defence of the archives, and the need for management of quantities of material, dictate that the background, context and provenance information about an entity has priority over detailed or case-by-case information.

In the Bagwith example (Figure 4.3), the macro and the micro

Level 3   1910–1924
    CDS1 Out-letters to district agencies.
           Sewn into card folders, each with index.
Level 4
    CDS1/1 7 Jan. 1910 – 4 Feb. 1911
        2 5 Feb. 1911 – 8 Mar. 1912 ...

Figure 4.4 Example of common information in a macro description

95

Group description, governing
Class description, governing
Item descriptions, etc.

Figure 4.5 Structure of a three-level finding aid

descriptions correspond fairly well with the descriptions appropriate to levels 2 and 4 respectively: but this correspondence is only fortuitous. There are two reasons why we cannot equate macro and micro with any specific level of arrangement.

The first reason is that the macro and micro relationship may exist at any level of arrangement. A macro description may be at level 4, governing descriptions at level 5; or it may be at level 1, giving headings which explain a set of group (micro) descriptions. Any combination can be visualized, provided only that the macro is at a higher level of arrangement than the micro. Multi-level combinations may also include more than two levels.

The second reason is that there are cases where the macro description does not correspond strictly to a level of arrangement. It is possible to visualize a set of descriptions, say at level 4, which are governed by a macro description specially written to govern them, which is not necessarily a description of the appropriate level 2 or 3.

In Figure 4.6, the macro description does not relate directly to the group to which most of the items belong, but was written specially to govern that particular set of item descriptions.

This introduces the concept of the *headnote*, which is an important one in MAD2. Headnotes are a common way to set out macro descriptions, since it is clear from the layout of the list that the headnote is intended to govern the material that is given beneath it. MAD2 makes it clear that this demonstration of the dependence of one section of a list (the micro descriptions) on another (the macro

Headnote	Falwell estate plans, 1794–1800		
	The following estate plans are drawn from the Smith of Falwell archive, except for TB/3, which originally belonged to that archive but was alienated at some time before 1900, and was recovered as part of a solicitor's papers (TB) in 1972.		
Micro	FE/3	Downton farm and nearby land	1794
description	FE/18	Small Wey and Downton	1799
	TB/3	Downton farm improvements	1800

Figure 4.6 A macro description spanning levels

descriptions) is an essential feature of archival finding aids, and is the way in which the multi-level rule generally operates.

Headnotes are not the only way of demonstrating dependence. MAD2 also visualizes the possibility of using title pages or title page sections to do the same job.

Using a title page simply means that the macro description, which is usually a title and a statement giving background, context and provenance, and common information, is given on a separate page, set immediately before the list containing the micro descriptions. This method is often most suitable when the micro list is very long, and is therefore best seen as a booklet or folder, complete in itself as a handling unit.

Where the macro description itself is very long, because the background information is complex, or there is a lot to say about the following material, then the title page may be expanded into a title page section. In this, the title page itself carries only such items as the repository name, and the overall title of the material to be described. The rest of the text of the macro description, including perhaps such things as a bibliography or notes and references, is given in succeeding pages. When all this has been written, the micro descriptions follow.

This discussion of the multi-level rule shows clearly the difference between levels of arrangement and levels of description. There is a correspondence between them, but levels of description also have their own characteristics.

Finding aids: management considerations

The general rule of archival description has already been mentioned. It is that description should proceed from the general to the particular. If there is no local reason to prevent it, archivists should generally complete the description of the group as a whole before dealing with descriptions of parts of the group. In particular, the practice of listing pieces or items first is discouraged. This is an application of the multi-level rule.

Since the materials have already been arranged into levels and into the various groupings that have emerged during analysis, it would be possible to begin the process of description either at the top (describing the whole entity, or the main collectivities in it), or at the bottom (describing individual items or pieces). As always in archives work, it is not possible to be completely dogmatic about this, since each case soon shows itself to be special, and archivists are not always in a position to do the ideal thing.

In general, it might be expected that management concerns will dictate that description should begin at the highest level, and work down. The need to manage the repository will certainly tend to suggest that whole groups should have a description made as early as possible, so that they can be found a place in storage, and entered into the guide. In practice, management requirements of this nature will probably recommend early completion of description down to class level. On the other hand, user demand (actual or anticipated) may cause archivists to give higher priority to completing descriptions of at least some of the items in a group. In fact it is possible to imagine cases where a group cannot seriously be controlled until there is a possibility of retrieval at levels 4 or 5. This might be the case, for example, where there was a mass of loose correspondence.

No doubt a management decision on this point would be taken in pragmatic terms. However, this discussion does give an opportunity to introduce some further general points about finding aids systems.

It is possible to perceive a difference in function between descriptions at levels at and above fractions of 2 (management groups, groups and subgroups), and those below this level. Particularly, there is a difference in function between descriptions of groups and descriptions at the level of item or below. (Class descriptions seem to occupy a variable place between these.)

The difference can be illustrated by tracing the actions of a user who comes into the repository in search of material. This person enters the repository and first consults the guide to holdings. If it is typical, this guide explains the division of material into management groups, and sets out a series of group, subgroup and class descriptions, together with an index. From this, the user can decide which classes might be relevant. She then goes into the reference room and, using the knowledge of classes obtained earlier, identifies which item lists refer to them. From these she is able to order specific items for production in the reading room. The user's objective has always been to find appropriate items, and it is these which are produced and read. At this stage, the information in the guide is only useful

    (a) as an explanation of how the repository is organized;

    (b) as a preliminary way of narrowing down the search.

However, there is another way in which the guide is valuable. It contains the background, contextual and provenance information which explains and gives meaning to the archives which are actually read: this is the physical manifestation of 'moral defence'. In actual practice, readers are only occasionally conscious that they have a need for background information of this kind. A reader who is consulting a parish register, for example, does not feel a need for any background information except the identity of the parish that the register belongs to: the other background information she needs is already present in the reader's experience – she knows what a parish is (or was), what a baptism is, and so on.

But in other cases much more information is needed. For example, if the reader is using a file of correspondence, it is necessary that somewhere some basic facts about its provenance are recorded: what organization did the file belong to, and what was the filing system used? Without the first of these bits of information it would be impossible to decide who was communicating with whom, and in what sequence. Without the second, it would be impossible to be sure whether that file contained all the relevant correspondence or not.

The user then must be able to refer to the background information, even though she may spend most of the time actually reading items. Looked at in this light, all descriptions containing background, context or provenance information function as one of the authority files of the archive service. It is possible to look at all descriptions at levels above level 3 as being essentially authorities: information linked to the finding aids proper, but called up from background when they are needed.

Class descriptions are in the middle position in the finding aids system. They have a structure which makes them look a bit like bibliographical descriptions, and this resemblance may be reinforced if they are kept in a flat file, like a card index. An important school of opinion in archival practice seeks to use the class level as the principal level of archival control. Class descriptions are not intelligible without the background information held in the relevant group or subgroup descriptions; and in turn the class descriptions govern the lists of items which belong to them.

All this builds up into a finding aids system. From the point of view of repository management, the finding aids have to be organized and located so that users can see their way around the system. The shelf

```
LCA-JHC/11                                              [1851] – 1941
Group: John Holt & Co. Ltd
Class: Photographs
Arrangement: In the catalogue the photographs have been given the following box
             numbers: 37–41 and 43. Photographs are listed under 8 subject
             headings: places; persons-European; persons-African; steamers; river
             vessels; miscellaneous; postcards; and negatives. Each photograph has
             been identified (where possible) by means of details in the photograph
             itself or from information found in the catalogue.
No. of items: c.1,100 photographs.

Structure:

[Reference Code (group/class)]
Group title
Class title
Content and character area information (free-text field)
Bulk/size and form
```

Source: Liverpool City Archives.

Figure 4.7 Example of a class description

layout, colour and style of the folders, notices, etc., should all be planned with this in mind. Traditionally, the repository guide, which generally contains group and class descriptions with an index, has been formally published. The more detailed lists and indexes, referring to items and below, have been held in the reference area. It seems likely that this pattern will be continued into the era of data exchange.

The data elements table

It is now necessary to discuss the structure of archival descriptions. It is important to understand the difference between a *field* and its *value*. Fields are spaces or categories set aside in order to be receptacles for certain types of information. Figure 4.7 gives an example of the description of a class, and shows that it is made up of (a) a more or less fixed structure of fields, and (b) information written in as contents to these fields. This information tells users about the nature and content of the class. The next class description will hold quite different information about another class; but it will have the same structure of fields. The same fields have been filled up with different data. When discussing this idea in the abstract, the information written into a field is termed its value.

The difference between fields and their values, and between a data structure (a set pattern of fields) and the set of descriptions which is built upon it, is a perfectly normal and everyday piece of understanding. Experience has shown that newcomers often become confused if this piece of theory is not explained at the outset. All archival descriptions are values held in a data structure. The precise shape of that structure depends not upon the data itself so much as upon the standard appropriate for the level of description, or the type of archive, etc. This is why it is so important that archivists should complete the development of suitable data standards for their work.

All descriptions, then, consist of data written into fields meant to contain just that kind of data. These fields are called *data elements*, and data elements are the irreducible bits of information which can be identified and labelled. MAD2 gives a full table of them, arranged

---

ARCHIVAL DESCRIPTION SECTOR

    Identity statement area*
        Reference code*
        Title*
            Term for form, type or genre
            Name element
            Simple span or bulk dates
        Level number

    Administrative and custodial history area
        Administrative history
        Custodial history

    Content and character area
        Abstract: summarizes content of the archive
        Diplomatic description: data on script, language etc.
        Physical description: size, bulk etc.

    Access, publication and reference area
        Access, copying, copyright, use in publication, related materials,
            exhibition or loan.

MANAGEMENT INFORMATION SECTOR (data not open to public)

    Administrative control information
        Acquisition or accession data
        Location

    Process control area
        Processing stages, production for reference, appraisal
            Conservation area: repair etc.

Figure 4.8 The data elements table

into logically connected sets (sectors, areas, sub-areas). A summary version of this table is as follows:

The data elements are divided into two sectors. The archival description sector contains information that is judged to be in the public domain. In principle, finding aids are published, or at least available for users; but as it is often necessary to keep some information private, a second sector has been provided for management information. Data held in the latter may be restricted to authorized users within the repository.

Data elements are also arranged into seven areas, which correspond to the main types of data. The use of the areas, and the sub-areas within them, is discussed in Chapter 5.

The international standard for archival description, ISAD(G), at first sight looks a little different. It contains 23 data elements, arranged into five areas:

1 Identity Statement Area
   [where essential information is conveyed to identify the unit of description]
   Title
   Dates of Creation of the Material in the Unit of Description
   Extent of Descriptive Unit (Quantity, Bulk or Size)
   Level of Description
2 Context and Content Area
   [where information is conveyed about the origin, arrangement, and subject matter of the unit of description]
   Administrative/Biographical History
   Custodial History
   Immediate Source of Acquisition
   Appraisal/Selection Information
   System of Arrangement
   Scope and Content Note/Abstract
   Dates of Accumulation of the Unit of Description
3 Condition of Access and Use Area
   [where information is conveyed about the availability of the unit of description]
   Language of Material
   Physical Characteristics
   Access Conditions
   Copyright/Terms Governing Reproduction
   Finding Aids

4 Allied Materials Area
   [where information is conveyed about materials having an important relationship to the unit of description]
   Location of Originals
   Existence of Copies
   Accrual Note
   Related Units of Description
   Associated Materials
5 Note Area
   [where specialized information is conveyed]

The two standards are aiming at different goals. MAD2 is intended to structure the finding aids system within a repository. Since that is also the intention of this book, a great deal of attention will be paid to it in this chapter. The aim of ISAD is to structure entries in a data exchange system, so that much more attention will be given to it in Chapter 6. The data elements of ISAD are given here, however, because they may assist an analysis of the information which has to go into an archival description in any context.

It is natural that the data elements in each standard should be similar, since all archival descriptions are variations on the same elements. An important question is whether the somewhat different ways in which the two standards arrange the data elements into areas is significant or not.

Archival descriptions are made up by choosing the most relevant model of a data structure, corresponding to the level of description, or to the format of the archive materials, or to the immediate circumstances of the work. This model presents a pattern of data elements, and it is then necessary to write in the information proper to each. Before setting out suitable models, the research team which eventually compiled the rules of MAD2 began by assembling all the possible data elements which might be used in a description.

When it came to writing out the list of data elements, it was found that they could be easily and naturally assembled in blocks: following the parallel of the *Anglo-American cataloguing rules* (AACR2), these were termed 'areas', and subdivisions were called (perhaps rather infelicitously) 'sub-areas'. At the end of the exercise, the table of data elements in MAD2 was found to contain seven areas, and 24 sub-areas. There were 83 data elements within these, but this number is not definitive as it is always possible that further elements will be added for the description of particular materials. The rules for the

103

REPOSITORY NAME	
IDENTITY STATEMENT	Level No.
Reference	Simple dates
Name	
ADMINISTRATIVE AND CUSTODIAL HISTORY	
CONTENT AND CHARACTER ABSTRACT	
PHYSICAL DESCRIPTION	Quantity
ACCESS, PUBLICATION AND REFERENCE	
MANAGEMENT INFORMATION	

Figure 4.9 Free-text form for description

description of special formats, included in MAD2, also have alternative tables of data elements.

In MAD2, the fact that the data elements are organized in areas and sub-areas is important because normally archivists would use these, rather than the individual data elements, when making up the descriptions to go into a finding aid. For example, the content and character area has three sub-areas, which describe different aspects of the original. These are the abstract (summary of content); diplomatic description; and physical description. Each sub-area may be broken down into individual data elements, but each deals with a whole aspect of the archive.

It was felt that the structure of sub-areas here would help describers by bringing forward these whole aspects, which would be completed by writing in the data in free-text style. Doing it this way allows the archivists much latitude in shaping the description. They can use blank paper, or forms in which the broad areas or sub-areas are simply sketched out, omitting unused fields.

In general, the free-text format suits archival descriptions which are being written at the work-place, especially if being done manually. The areas and sub-areas are usually convenient to give some basic structure and uniformity, while allowing archivists considerable freedom to write in textual description.

In other cases, descriptions need an even more strongly structured format. This would be so where very formal or legal documents were being dealt with, or where the description had to be composed or transcribed by clerical staff. These descriptions could be analysed down into individual data elements, each of which could be given a dedicated field, if this was thought necessary. Computerized systems often work by presenting screen spaces for each data element, so for these there had to be a well-defined model.

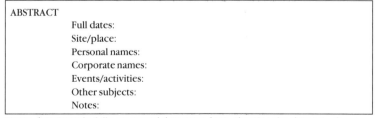

ABSTRACT
        Full dates:
        Site/place:
        Personal names:
        Corporate names:
        Events/activities:
        Other subjects:
        Notes:

Figure 4.10 Part of a fully structured data entry form, showing the abstract sub-area

When this fully structured approach is being used, the opportunity for using free text and vocabulary will be minimized. Entries in the fields in a form such as Figure 4.10 are best treated as formal access points, subject to authority control.

Description: general principles

MAD2 has several general rules and some guidelines, which should be available to help archivists with the preparation of their finding aids.

1 Most data elements are optional

Except for something to identify the material being described, no area, sub-area or data element is obligatory in the context of any one description. Anything may be left out of a description except an identifier. The full identity statement area includes reference code, the title sub-area (which can contain a form/type/genre element, a name element and a simple date), and, to be quite complete, a note of the level number. It is sufficient in any real description to give only one of these: the reference code, or only the name element of the title. Everything else can be left out, if that is what is wanted. Empty areas simply do not appear.

There have been several attempts to provide a model for a minimum description.[5] Obviously an archival description which contains only a reference code is not going to be very useful for a wide range of purposes. It is a representation, but not one which has any obvious general function. The rule is there to give emphasis to the principle that one does not have to use every data element or every area or sub-area in a description. Only those which are actually

(a) *A full statement*

Hoylake Record Office DWB	
Birket Water Board archives, 1899–1910	[Level 2]

(b) *An identity statement sufficient for most purposes*

Hoylake Record Office DWB
or
Birket Water Board archives

Figure 4.11 Examples of identity statements

relevant at the moment should be used; but an identity statement must always be one of them.

Minimum descriptions may be useful in cases where resources are scarce and where it is immediately necessary to contribute to a data exchange system, or to put material into use. In the same way, it would be desirable to secure agreement on rules and models for an optimum description. The great variety of forms that archives can take, and the complication of multiple levels, has so far prevented the emergence of these standards.

2 Data elements are not fixed to particular levels

Any area, sub-area or data element may be used at any level of description, if it is relevant. Thus although the administrative and custodial history area is specially characteristic of descriptions of groups, it is possible to find group descriptions which leave this area out. In the same way, it is not difficult to find item descriptions which do have an administrative and custodial history area.

This rule has in its time caused much trouble to the MAD2 researchers, because it makes it difficult to devise models proper to the levels of arrangement. For example, it is impossible to say that group descriptions are always in free text, or that item descriptions always consist of brief tabulated entries.

Also, the interpretation of data elements alters as we move from level to level. Physical descriptions of groups, for example, deal with generalities, but physical descriptions of items are specific. Information concerning preservation needs is also specific for small quantities, where it can be used to help control repair processes. When it comes to the preservation of large groups, the conservation area relates much more to environmental or preventative conservation, although still often needed. This feature of archival description marks it out strongly from bibliographic description, and it is important that archivists should understand the difference.

3 The length of text in data elements is variable

Data elements should not, in principle, be restricted in length or content. It is true that specific page layouts may demand that some data elements should be given in dedicated fields of restricted size. Thus the identity statement which appears at the head of most descriptions might have three dedicated fields: reference code, title and simple date. In some repositories, there may be a rule that this title should extend across the middle of a page. If there is a rule like this, then there must be a consequential restriction on the amount of text which can be put into the field. However, this is a local rule, and does not affect the general principle. It has been adopted simply to ensure that the description that comes below the title is identifiable and comprehensible.

Particular computer applications, in the same way, may include field restrictions which are part of the design of the database. But otherwise, restrictions should not be obtrusive. It is important that archivists should not be unnecessarily constrained in writing their descriptions and setting them out.

Where the information which constitutes one of the free-text entries, such as the administrative and custodial history sub-area or the abstract sub-area, is written out in narrative form, the constituent data elements may be marked out within the text by tags or side headings, if this is helpful. This, in effect, makes these elements into subfields.

Some computer systems[6] contain lists of data elements in 'templates': these are formatted screens which can be called up to help with listing archival (or other special) materials. Highly structured displays like these may be helpful where very formal descriptions are being given, for example where strings of keywords must be included. In other cases the archivist's freedom of expression should be valued, and the free-text approach retained. The data element analysis may be used to help archivists to include all relevant information, but should not be used to impose too rigid a structure. This recommendation is directed especially at those who are designing a data capture form for use within an archives service.

A liberal approach towards free text in description is typical of MAD2, which was intended primarily as a guide to manually constructed finding aids. If the description is to be entered into a shared database, however, much more restriction has to be accepted. MAD2 also provides for this, where relevant. The most extreme case will presumably be where a MARC format is being used for entry to an electronic database. This will be dealt with in Chapter 6.

The shape of descriptions at different levels

Descriptions are made up by selecting the areas, sub-areas and/or data elements which are to be used, and fitting these together in accordance with one of the models which are given below, or with a model set out in a house style by the repository.

MAD2 gives a model for each level of description. The clarity and decisiveness that might have been conveyed by the apparent hard edges of these models, are blurred by the possibility of choice between alternative modes of description – paragraph and list modes.

Modes of description

Paragraph mode descriptions are used when there is a lot of text, which is then written in a central block occupying the middle of the page.

List mode descriptions are arranged in tabulated columns down the page; usually at least one of these columns contains text, but of limited length.

The difference between these two modes is clear, and many examples of each can be found in repository practice. However, in real life any particular description may fall between the two or may form a hybrid. The two modes are none the less needed because they allow alternative models to be proposed to structure description in different cases.

A good model for description should allow for a choice of mode at any level. In practice, descriptions down to level 3 arc likely to be in paragraph mode, and those below 3 are likely to be in list mode: but there are many exceptions, and the choice of mode (or of an intermediate form) must exist at any level. Choosing a mixture of modes in the same finding aid must also be allowed as a possibility. It sounds undesirable, but in practice the form of an archival description is largely determined by what has to be said in it.

Management group headings (level 1)

Descriptions at management group level are termed 'headings'. This is because the function of these groupings is more to help with the management of the repository and with giving broad guidance to users, than with the description of actual archival entities. Typically they appear as headnotes to group descriptions. Level 1 headings give the administrative and legal background to the creation of the relevant groups. Narrative like this normally demands paragraph treatment.

The Education Act 1870 authorized the formation of school boards to establish or take over responsibility for schools in areas of inadequate educational provision. The functions and property of school boards were transferred to local education authorities in 1903. The county had 22 school boards, the work of some being continued after 1903 by reappointing existing boards of managers of individual schools.

Source: Gloucestershire Record Office.

Figure 4.12 An example of a level 1 heading

This type of entry, consisting mainly of background, context and provenance information, can be of great value to some users, but is not needed by others. These descriptions should contain access points, by which users can effectively begin their search. Sets of administrative histories like the one above can also be treated as authority files, to be called on when required. Sets of level 1 administrative histories could be incorporated into the authority system used in a repository.

Examples of level 1 headings occurring as list mode entries can also be found, especially where the finding aid is giving an overview of

CHESHIRE RECORD OFFICE
[Address, opening hours, user information]
The principal groups of archives are:
County Council archives, 1888–
    Architecture
    Education
    Fire prevention
    Health
    Highways and transportation
    Libraries
    Planning   [Second column available
    Police   for summary information]
    Secretariat
    Social Services
    Treasury
Private and family archives
Ecclesiastical archives
    Diocese of Chester
    Chester Cathedral
    Quakers (Society of Friends)

Source: Cheshire Record Office.

Figure 4.13 Level 1 headings in list mode

repository holdings. In this case the repository name and descriptive details themselves might form a headnote governing the list of management groups.

The example in Figure 4.13 shows that list mode descriptions cannot usually be used as macro descriptions, because the tabular format does not favour setting out one description as governing others. As always there is an important exception to this rule. Where the finding aid is multi-level it is possible to find cases where descriptions occurring in a tabulated list are interspersed with subordinate descriptions at a level below.

As Figure 4.13 shows, it is possible to have any number of intermediate levels in the general category of management groups. Subgroups formed like this can be numbered by using decimal fractions of 1.

Group descriptions (level 2)

In exactly the same way as with level 1, level 2 descriptions done at any depth naturally tend to be set in paragraph mode. Their essential function is to record the background, context and provenance of groups and to outline the classes which fall within them. This is normally done by giving prominence to the administrative and custodial history area, which is naturally expressed in narrative.

Identity statement:		
Ref. code	Title	Simple dates

Administrative and custodial history area:
[Explains the origin, structure, functions and development of the organization which created the group, and the sequence of custodial arrangements for it, ending with transfer to the archives service.]

Content and character of the whole group:
[Gives information on the data held in the group as a whole, and on the physical character of the major components. An important feature may be a description of the way the group is arranged, noting the relationships between subgroups, and the classes which belong to each.]

Figure 4.14 Level 2 descriptions

```
Level 1
        Businesses
Level 2
                JR Cave Ltd, Chemists, Southport, 1936-1965
                Garston Land Co. (Garston Bottle Works), 1868-1974
Level 1
        Estates
Level 2
                Legh of Newton-le-Willows, 1870-1950
```

Source: Merseyside County Archives.

Figure 4.15 Level 2 description in list mode

Another important component would be the content and character area, which also tends to appear most naturally in blocks of text.

This type of group description has a model such as that in Figure 4.14.

Most of this material would normally be written out as narrative. At the end of this there may be a list of the subgroups, and additional material such as a bibliography, topical headings or index.

In the model in Figure 4.14, a distinction can be noted between the three fields in the heading, and the large blocks of text which come below it. The fields in the heading are dedicated fields, because their contents are strictly defined, and their length and setting on the page are determined by this definition. The others are free-text fields: their content is defined in looser terms (typically allocating them as space for areas or sub-areas), but not restricted in length or format. It is an essential feature of the MAD2 system that free-text fields should not be arbitrarily restricted in length or wording. The distinction between these two kinds of field is maintained in all the description models.

Group descriptions also occur in list mode as part of a repository guide or overview. Tabulated columns to contain the reference code, title sub-area and simple dates would form a natural and commonly occurring finding aid for groups.

Subgroup descriptions

Subgroups are much less easy to model, because they can occur in a variety of different roles. Subgroups can hardly be seen as indepen-

```
READY-MADE & WHOLESALE BESPOKE TAILORING TRADE BOARD
[Level 2]
The Trade Boards Act 1909 set up boards empowered to fix minimum wage rates
in certain unorganized trades, such as clothing, where public feeling had been
aroused against 'sweated wages'. The group includes the following:
[Level 2.5]
      Corset Trade Board, 1919-1926,
         including discussion of scope and definition of the trade.
      Shirt-making Trade Board, 1914-1919.
      Tailoring Trade Board, 1910-1925.
```

Source: Modern Records Centre, University of Warwick.

Figure 4.16 Descriptions at levels 2 and 2.nn

```
              ARCHIVES OF THE SCOTTISH COLLEGE OF COMMERCE
                     These are divided into two subgroups:
                ROYAL SCOTTISH ACADEMY OF MUSIC AND DRAMA
Previously the Glasgow Athenaeum; deposited October 1979. This subgroup
contains the earliest commercial archives, 1847-c.1900.
      Minute books of the Glasgow Athenaeum
            1                    1847-1851
            2                    1851-1859
                  SCOTTISH COLLEGE OF COMMERCE
The SCC had two institutional antecedents, the Athenaeum Commercial College
and the Glasgow and West of Scotland Commercial College, c.1900-1964.
            Account Books
```

Source: Based on material in Strathclyde University Archives.

Figure 4.17 Description at level 2.nn as headnote

dent from the group to which they belong. This is the reason why they do not have a level number of their own; in fact, if a subgroup is sufficiently different from other parts of the archive as to suggest that it might be described independently, then it probably should be treated as a group on its own. However, despite this lack of independence, subgroup descriptions in practice often act as macro descriptions governing sets of classes. Consequently, subgroup descriptions can be found in two distinct roles.

When the subgroup description appears as a part of the group description, it will tend to look like a section of the overall macro description provided for the group.

The second form in which subgroup descriptions can occur is

113

Identity statement:			
Ref. code	Title sub-area		Simple dates
Quantity/bulk		Form/type/genre	
Content and character area (free text; other areas as needed)			

Figure 4.18 Model for a level 3 description

HLG36   Central Housing Advisory Committee minutes and papers 1935–1955   31 files   Files of correspondence and papers of the MINISTRY OF HEALTH and the   MINISTRY OF HOUSING AND LOCAL GOVERNMENT relating to the   constitution and operation of the Committee and its sub-committees, copies of   minutes and papers of the Committee and bound volumes of its signed minutes.

Source: Public Record Office, Crown Copyright.

Figure 4.19 An example of a level 3 description in paragraph mode

when they carry out the role of macro description governing class or item lists. In this case they have a model similar to that of the group.

There are probably other cases, where subgroups are treated in a different way. In general, descriptions may be put into list mode where it is desired to provide an overview. Whichever mode, or whatever format, is used, the dependence of subgroups on their group should always be emphasized.

Class descriptions (level 3)

Although class descriptions, like all others, can be set out in either mode, they characteristically show a tendency towards paragraph mode. Even so, it would be normal for these descriptions to use a relatively strongly defined structure. The model for class descriptions in this mode contains more dedicated fields than in any other.

Class descriptions may appear in list mode, especially in guides or finding aids which provide an overview of holdings. There is another situation in which list mode class descriptions are common: this is where they act as subordinate headnotes within a more comprehensive finding aid.

1/3/	*Cash books*	1882–1942
	The cash books are of value in revealing much of the internal organization of the firm. They show, for example, the proportions of the work carried out by each of the partners, and the names of the employees in the drawing office.	
	3 vols	
	[Level 4:]	
	1	1882–1889
	2	1889–1914

Source: Gloucestershire Record Office.

Figure 4.20 Level 3 descriptions in list mode.

In this situation, within a list, MAD2 recommends that the class title should be underlined or italicized, in order to emphasize its function as a headnote for what follows. The rule is not absolute, since underlinings within a list are not always desirable.

If class descriptions are used as the basic control instrument, then related group and subgroup descriptions should be linked. Users would be able to call them up when information on background, context and provenance was required. This principle is probably best observed in a computerized finding aids system.

In Australian practice, class (series) descriptions are consciously taken as the essential central level of archival management. This example should be followed by archives services which have serious trouble with continuing accruals of material in organizations which have a constantly changing administrative structure. The problem is that while departmental boundaries and functional competence may often change, the actual administrative functions tend to continue uninterrupted. Records arising from particular functions continue to accrue to existing classes. These classes are then transferred to the archives, under regular management procedures. Archivists then have the difficulty of explaining to their users the complex background of these records. If the group or subgroup is taken as the starting-point for description, then one of these situations will arise:

(a) classes are described as belonging to departments which are historically incorrect;

(b) class descriptions are broken up into different departments;

(c) cross-references become complex and intrusive.

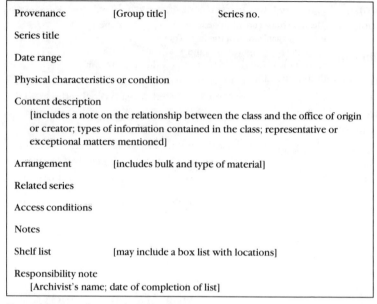

Provenance	[Group title]	Series no.

Series title

Date range

Physical characteristics or condition

Content description
   [includes a note on the relationship between the class and the office of origin
   or creator; types of information contained in the class; representative or
   exceptional matters mentioned]

Arrangement   [includes bulk and type of material]

Related series

Access conditions

Notes

Shelf list   [may include a box list with locations]

Responsibility note
   [Archivist's name; date of completion of list]

Figure 4.21 Australian standard class description sheet

The solution adopted by Australian archivists is to describe all classes as if they were independent, and to provide background, context and provenance information partly in the class description itself, and partly in group descriptions held in a common reference facility – these group descriptions then act, in effect, as authority files.

As a consequence of adopting this policy, Australian archivists have been able to establish a national standard for class (series) descriptions.[7]

An examination of this worksheet will quickly reveal how close it is to the MAD2 model, which was designed independently. (MAD2 provides for the inclusion of any additional field that might be useful, for example a note on access conditions). The most important difference, in principle, is that in the Australian model, the group title must always precede the class title, and thus forms part of it. In the MAD2 approach, this would not be regarded as necessary because it visualizes all class descriptions as appearing under the general (macro) heading of a group description, which of course contains a title. It would be perfectly possible for a standard class description

116

form to be devised for use in other countries, which would be compatible with the Australian form.

Item and piece descriptions (level 4)

At these levels the norm changes from paragraph to list mode, although both forms are often encountered. Most typical is the model presented by a tabulated list set out below a paragraph mode headnote.

The model does not specify what the field names (column headings) should be: they should be chosen to display the information needed in the particular case. Three or four columns are common, but there is no restriction on the number or width of columns, other than those imposed by the width of the page.

In the model shown, the title column would contain free text, and no maximum length for this is specified in the rules. Clearly the writer's scope will be restricted by the requirements of the columnar layout (very long text squeezed into a column could be unpleasing and wasteful). Length of text can be reduced to some extent if some of the information can be given in the headnote. This is certainly the recommended practice where such information is common to more than one item or piece. MAD2 discourages unnecessary repetition of data in items governed by a headnote.

The Archival Description Project, researching for the first edition of MAD, found that about 40% of lists customarily placed the date column on the left centre of the page (in the position occupied by the 'Former code' column in Figure 4.22. Although MAD2 states constantly that each archives service should set its own model (within the general framework of the standard), and that house styles should be

Headnote: macro description in free text			
Column headings (field names):			
Ref. code	Former code	Title	Date

Figure 4.22 Model for level 4 descriptions

117

Identity statement:		
Ref. code	Item (piece) title	Simple date

Content and character area
  Abstract
    Data elements of abstract		

Diplomatic description [elements may be given dedicated fields]		
Physical description		

Figure 4.23 Level 4 descriptions in list mode

[Level 2:]

                       HOWELL-JONES PARTNERSHIP

    DHJ   1794-1910

    Founded in 1794 by William Howell in Saltborough as a
brokering business...
The archives of two departments survive: General Manager's
and Finance Controller.

[Level 2.5:]

                          GENERAL MANAGER

    DHJ/GM   1892-1910

    Consists mainly of the daily reports of market operations, in
a series of leather-bound volumes. Some subsidiary files
exist for the period 1900-1910.

[Level 3:]

    GM1   *Daily reports*   1892-1900

            150 volumes, indexed. Reports on market rates
and conditions in text, statistics in columns

[Level 4:]

            /1 (hardly legible; water damage)   1892

            2   1893

Figure 4.24 Multi-level descriptions

followed, it is a consistent feature of its guidelines that dates should
appear in the right margin, to assist users to scan for them.

Item or piece lists may also be given in paragraph mode, and if
there is a lot of text, this would be the preferred way. Suitable models
might be found in the practice of many repositories (it has been
customary to describe title deeds in this way, for example). It is

Guide: Management level headings with summary lists of groups
        Groups, subgroups

Reference area: Classes
        Indexes

Reading room: Item/piece lists
        Indexes

Figure 4.25 Model for a finding aids system

somewhat more usual to have more dedicated fields than in descriptions at the higher levels.

Fitting levels together in a finding aid

Owing to the operation of the multi-level rule, archival finding aids normally contain at least two levels, and often three or four. A good illustration is provided by the catalogue of a group.

If it were fully worked out, and if it were to include an index, this example would conform to the MAD2 definition of a catalogue, because it contains in a single finding aid, descriptions of all the main levels of one group. Group catalogues of this kind, or variations not too far from the model, are very common.

However, the question might be asked whether it would not be better to build up finding aids systems by linking together a larger number of more specific finding aids. Instead of a catalogue for each group, it might be preferable to put all the group descriptions together to act as a set of authority files. The class descriptions would also be kept separately, to form the first access points for most users. They would direct users to sets of item/piece descriptions, from which documents could be ordered up to the reading room. This is done in the classic scheme for a finding aids system, built up on the model shown in Figure 4.25.

In a multi-level finding aid, the layout of the page is important. It is necessary to set out the material so as to demonstrate how micro descriptions depend on their macro descriptions. Figure 4.25 demonstrates that this is mainly done using one or both of two devices:

   (a) adjusting the spaces between blocks of text, and especially between distinct descriptions. This makes clear to the user when one begins and another ends, and how one block relates to the one above or below it;

119

Borsetshire Record Office
EMF/R1/   6
             7
             8
      R2/1   etc.

Figure 4.26 Sequence of reference codes on the page

(b) adjusting the right and left margins. Generally, both margins should be narrower in a micro description than in the macro description that governs it. Narrowing the margins in this way allows dependence to be seen, and it can be repeated down a sequence of three or more levels. The only restriction is of course the need to keep a line long enough to contain all the text that is required.

On the left margin the reference code should appear. It is recommended that the full code should be given at least once on each page, at the head of the left column. Specific reference codes which follow should be given in the appropriate place, the character column below the main code, as in Figure 4.26.

It is sometimes contended that the needs of users dictate that the full reference (or at least an adequate call number) should appear next to each entry in a finding aid. MAD2 allows this, in cases where the needs of the repository are better served by it, and (what would seem to be the same thing) where the result is clearer for the user.

Textual fields should occupy the centre of the page, and naturally should be given as long a line as possible, within the requirements of the character columns on each side.

The right margin is generally reserved for simple dates, in both paragraph and list modes. The purpose of this guideline is to assist scanning for date information. Users can pick up relevant dates quickly by running their eye down the page. Complex or very exact dates should be repeated in their full form in the textual part of the description. Dates in the right column should always be kept simple, ideally a four-figure year date, or a range between two four-figure year dates, if this is possible.

MAD2 recommends that archivists should write in the level number next to each description. This piece of data is not directly of interest to the user, and may be confusing, so the recommendation is that the level number should be written in a distinctive colour, or perhaps

```
Class description as headnote
        (one blank line)

First item description
Second item description
        (two blank lines)

Class description as headnote ... etc.
```

Figure 4.27 Displaying level relationships

restricted to the finding aids used by internal staff. Writing in the level number is a practice which helps archivists to analyse their material correctly.

The space which follows each description in a composite finding aid should be adjusted to emphasize the relationships displayed in the finding aid.

Page layout is clearly of great importance in composite finding aids. The result should be simple and clear. The MAD2 standard should produce widespread common practice which will help users and be conducive to practical schemes for data exchange between repositories. Repositories may find it useful to consider using a mark-up convention to help them with organizing page layouts.

Mark-up conventions are commonly available today as part of word-processing or print preparation packages. It is recommended, however, that a general standard should be adopted, and this should be the *Standard generalized mark-up language* (SGML). If this is used to mark page layout, typeface and the hierarchy of headings, the exchange of texts and their output in different formats will be made much easier.

Special cases: indexes as finding aids

Certain kinds of archival material demand the use of indexes as a basic finding aid. There are three examples:

- long series of minutes or proceedings of corporate bodies
- correspondence
- self-indexing documents, e.g. wills.

1 Series of minutes or proceedings

An index is required here because listing the physical items is not useful. The meetings themselves would normally deal with all the subjects with which the organization in question had to deal. For example, the minutes of Cabinet meetings contain the record of discussions and decisions on all subjects faced by the government at the time. Despite this, an item list can only say something like:

Minute book, July 1932–Aug. 1933. Indexed.

Such a list is useful only to those enquirers who have a clear idea of the date at which the decision they are interested in occurred. Otherwise, their only resource is to browse. An index can bring out the necessary references to events, subjects, persons and documents.

2 Correspondence

In a similar way, a series of letters contains a range of subjects corresponding to the range of interests of the correspondents. The item list could hardly do more than list the names of correspondents and the date coverage applicable to each. There are only two ways to get closer to the actual data. One way is to transcribe or calendar the letters, and this is often done; the other is to index directly to the contents of the original. This is done in the British Library Manuscripts Department, but is not common elsewhere.

3 Self-indexing series

These can range from those which can only be accessed by using the indexing key, such as case files arranged in a numerical system, to those which are bundled on some principle such as alphabetical or chronological. It is generally necessary to improve the indexing principle. Thus with wills, one must extract the names of wills in sessional bundles and arrange the list alphabetically.

Notes and references:

1 Report of the Working Group on Standards for Archival Description, published in *The American archivist*, **52**, 1989, 442.
2 The first edition – Cook, M. and Grant, K., *A manual of archival description* (British Library R&D Report 5867) – was published by the Society of Archivists, 1985. The second (current) edition (Cook, M. and Procter, M., British Library R&D Report 5965) was published by Gower, 1990. The principles laid down in MAD1

were maintained in MAD2, but the rules were made more extensive and specific.

3 At the time of writing, this is available as International Council on Archives, Ad Hoc Commission on Archival Description, *Working document 2: draft ISAD(G): General international standard archival description*. Prepared for the Secretariat, Ottawa, Canada, November 1991.

4 Jenkinson, C.H., *A manual of archive administration*, 2nd edn (revised), Lund Humphries, 1965, 128ff.

5 It has been argued that a minimum description must contain some content information, and not merely a statement that the material is there and can be found. This debate may be resolved during the formulation of the international standards.

6 Such as the Museum Documentation Association's MODES (Archival Description). Practice in this system can be demonstrated by the MODES user group of the Society of Archivists Information Technology Group.

7 Pederson, A. (ed.), *Keeping archives*, Australian Society of Archivists, Sydney, 1987, 148.

5

The retrieval and use of information

Archives and records are information media. They have their own special needs and characteristics, but the management and exploitation of these materials demand the use of tools which belong to the general field of information management, and to the body of theory known as information science. This is particularly easy to see when we come to consider the retrieval and use of the information in our system.

The successful exploitation of any complex source of information demands some expertise in two areas: the techniques of information retrieval, and the study of user needs. It is a curious fact that few archival training courses in the past have given much attention to either. As a consequence, few archivists in post have much knowledge of the technical tools available in either field. The arrival of IT has made it clear that this is a problem for the professional body, and that some remedies will have to be found.

Techniques of information retrieval

Not all the theory, and not every technique, developed by information scientists is necessarily applicable to the work of records managers or archivists. However, some parts of this body of knowledge are essential. The most relevant areas of knowledge are as follows:

- a grounding in communications and information theory
- computer literacy
- techniques of information retrieval, especially
    cataloguing rules and practice
    indexing and classification theory and practice
    the use of authorities
    theory and practice of online searching of databases and texts

- the analysis of user needs
- the provision of user services.

Communications and information theory

This aspect of professional training was discussed briefly in Chapter 1. Since there is already a considerable specialist literature available, only those aspects directly relevant to archives and records management are considered here.

General

The whole process whereby the information resources of an archives service are brought together with the information needs of users is the subject of study by information scientists. The body of theory which they have produced, and the battery of technologies which they have developed, should be available for adaptation in the training of archivists and records managers.

In the context of information retrieval and use, several aspects of archive administration practice overlap each other and need to be well linked.

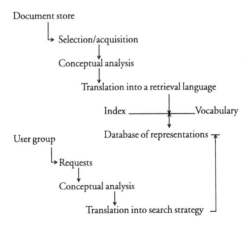

Figure 5.1 The information retrieval problem

At this point we are chiefly interested in what happens during the phases designated as conceptual analysis and translation:

(a) conceptual analysis of document holdings: this is a process which occurs during arrangement and description. It involves:

    (i)   policy – the repository must have a guideline on the depth to which finding aids will be constructed;

    (ii) support and infrastructural resources: authority lists and guidelines; also training support;

    (iii) the construction of satisfactory representations.

(b) translation into a retrieval language: this involves the selection of terms, and setting them into a context in which they can be appreciated and used by the various user groups.

(c) conceptual analysis of user requests: this includes the capture of these requests, which may be done through a system, including remote systems, or through an interview. There is a body of experience in and a literature covering both of these.

(d) translation into a search strategy: this involves analysing the user's request and turning it into a form which, while remaining true, is compatible with the language and instruments of the finding aids system.

All this may sound rather laborious, but it has in some manner to be done. If there is a lack of fit between the ideas of the user and the concepts presented in the finding aids, then the right documents will not be found. It would be like the work of tunnelling engineers who have not calculated exactly the point at which the drills from the two ends would meet – amusing for the onlookers but disastrous for those responsible.

Records management

In RM, there are several useful technologies and strategies available. These include learning and using the central information system to build in an additional set of channels. On the document store side these include:

- Information on records held (the register of classes)
- Information on how to use the system, both to transfer documents and to retrieve them.

On the user side, they include:

- Personal profiles of the principal users, so that proactive steps can be taken to supply information as it becomes available
- Consultation with principal users on appraisal and disposal of records
- Use of classification theory for making filing indexes, including those for email files.

The interface between all these can be set up by adapting and extending the organization's information systems.

Archives management

There are some differences between RM and archival management, in this context.

On the document store side, the universe of knowledge represented is likely to be much wider. In RM, document retrieval is often by class or file, using known references, and working within the range of departmental functions. In archives, the information held in the materials is controlled at a deeper level, which means that intellectual controls are needed, and that a wealth of information on unexpected subjects is likely to be uncovered. It is likely that informational values are prominent, rather than evidential ones, and these values are often unpredictable.

On the user request side, it is probably much less easy to define the interests of all user groups. Methods of analysis of what groups there are and of what their real needs might be will involve many more of the technologies of social science.

Between these two there is a more complicated interface which brings into question the design of the user services, both remote and local, and of the finding aids system.

Computer literacy

This summary of a range of activities shows very clearly that practitioners should understand what parts of the service can benefit from automation, and how to go about implementing an automated service. It is now well understood that no information management system can succeed without the power of computers to process and communicate information.

What is meant by 'computer literacy'? A first attempt to answer this question might be to define the negative: what is *not* meant by it? It is agreed nowadays, among archivists at least, that it is not necessary to be trained in programming. Still less is there a need for technical knowledge of electronics and computer operation. Neither of these perceptions were so obvious in the past as they are today. This was because in the early days of practical computing it was more necessary to build one's own system from scratch. Those who wrote their own programs in the early 1970s may today be given honour as courageous pioneers, but in this period of abundant predesigned software packages, their painfully acquired knowledge can be seen as no longer relevant, perhaps even misleading. Even the programming languages they used are probably not currently the most useful.

Armed with this observation, we can look for a more positive answer to the question. Since it is now clear that we should use existing technologies as the basis of our system, the essential knowledge should be in the professional area rather than in the technical. Archivists and records managers should be able to analyse their work problems and translate this analysis into a system specification. This specification can then be discussed with technical suppliers, and costed. After that, there will be a test period in which there is close consultation between the two sides. Finally a maintenance relationship develops.

This is the context in which the IT Group of the Society of Archivists produced its guidelines for the computer element in basic professional training.[1]

Computer literacy for archives and records professionals should certainly go further than an understanding of their own professional needs and aims. It should include enough technical knowledge to enable them to evaluate the externals, at least, of a computer system intelligently. They should have a broad understanding of hardware (processors and peripherals), software (operating systems and applications), communications and terminology. A practical yardstick would be that they should understand and be interested in the computer page of a respectable newspaper; and they should be accustomed to use public teletext services. This level of understanding, backed by experience, will be enough to allow them to converse intelligibly (and with authority within their own field) with technical experts and suppliers.

Another way of explaining the level of knowledge required is by comparing applications software packages with operating systems. It is possible to make a software package work without knowing anything about the operating system that it works with; rather in the way that one can use a car for work without realizing that it has differential gears. However, users of software packages will be working in a very restricted mode if they do not understand the nature of a file, the way files are managed together in directories, and how to carry out some useful manipulatory functions on them. A user who cannot independently copy a group of files to make a back-up disk, for example, is one who probably does not take adequate precautions against data loss. So archivists ought to be able to use the facilities offered by their operating system (DOS, UNIX, etc.), and should be able to consider the relative values of systems short-listed under their specification.

Cataloguing rules and practice

The role of cataloguing rules is well defined in the library world. The application of description rules in archival management was given a general explanation in Chapter 4, and will be discussed again in the context of data exchange (Chapter 6).

There are two areas in which description rules apply. The MAD2 rules concern the writing of finding aids, which support the administrative and intellectual management of archival materials in a repository. The other rules available (APPM2, RAD, ISAD) deal with the construction of 'bibliographic' descriptions which are either for public presentation outside the repository's reading room or for data exchange, or both. The two purposes are interlinked, of course.

Access points

The international standard, ISAD(G), and the library-influenced cataloguing rules, APPM and RAD, all provide for the construction of access points, which they assume are essential features of (exchangeable) archival descriptions. MAD2 does not use the term 'access point', but instead has a rule which is intended to ensure that searchable terms should appear in every text.[2]

The concept that underlies the designation of access points belongs strictly to library practice. The catalogue description of a book has a heading at the top which gives a main distinguishing feature of the item. The description can then be repeated under different headings until all the main descriptors have been used. The usual main heading is an author's name, but other names, subject terms, titles etc. can also be used. Archival descriptions use the idea of a main heading, at least to some extent, by writing in a title to each unit of description. The concept of access points can also be used, if each significant name or term can be successively extracted and put into a searchable place. Users could then scan the descriptions until they find a relevant term, which is then effectively the point at which they can gain useful access to the finding aids.

An important feature of access points is that they should be subject to authority controls. This means that names of persons or corporate bodies should be set out strictly according to rule.[3] Where an authority list of names exists, new entries should use a form that is already there; new entries may only be made subject to authorization. If the authorities extend to subject terms (there are obvious difficulties about this, but in an ideal world they should be), the terms should be arranged in logical hierarchies of meaning, as in a thesaurus. These measures should ensure that searches are not frustrated because the searcher has used the wrong term.

As a generalization, finding aids should follow either the MAD2 rule, which aims to provide a suitable target for any search within the text of a description, or the ISAD(G) rule, which provides access points that users may scan. Either approach demands at least some degree of vocabulary control.

Indexing and classification theory and practice

Despite discussion of the topic in professional circles, none of the archival training schools in Britain yet formally teaches the principles and practice of indexing or classification. Historically, the present practice represents a step backwards, for indexing, at least, was once taught, but in connection with editing methods. Now that editing documentary texts is regarded as principally the business of historians or literary researchers, indexing has tended to drop from the syllabus. At the same time, more general approaches to the subject developed by departments of information studies have not been taken up, and in any case course syllabuses are increasingly overcrowded. It is urgently necessary that a bridge should be built between archival training courses and other mainstream training in information work, in this area of information retrieval.

In archive practice, the importance of indexing has varied

considerably from one period to another. Apart from the indexes required by published full texts and calendars, it has generally been treated as relatively unimportant. The great national repositories like the British Library and the Bodleian Library have continued to use indexes as a principal means of access to large collections. Elsewhere, indexes have tended to play a secondary role. It has been common for archives services to use them simply as means of access to peripheral materials, such as printed sources acquired for the repository library, or as a retrieval aid appended to published lists.

Index planning

Indexes are an essential part of a finding aids system. In this context they are known generically as *retrieval aids*. MAD2 recommends that they should normally refer primarily to the relevant finding aid, rather than directly to originals; but there are cases where it is better to index directly.

Most finding aids need a retrieval aid, as an initial access point, in order to help users to start their access trails.

Unless the scope of the index is limited by the nature of the job it performs, indexes tend naturally to grow and become unwieldy. Many indexes are naturally limited in scope and size: for example, the index which appears at the back of a volume, or the index to a closed group of materials. Once these indexes have covered their materials, they remain static, and since it is not usually desired to merge them together, it may not matter too much if they are not totally compatible with each other.

In other cases, where there are no natural limitations, indexes tend to continue being enlarged because the material they refer to continues to be indexed. Very large indexes show planning defects very clearly, and in the worst cases become unusable. Also, where indexes arc developed separately, there is always the possibility of merging them into a union index. As soon as this possibility is examined, inconsistencies and duplications become depressingly obvious, and become increasingly important as barriers to successful operation of the service.

Questions of vocabulary control arise early and ought to be settled at the planning stage. As with the finding aids themselves, there is a choice between using natural language and adopting a controlled vocabulary. The case for controlling the entries is much stronger and more obvious with an index than with text; indeed the index may be the way in which a controlled vocabulary is adapted to a natural-language text. The best way of controlling vocabulary in an index is by using a thesaurus, which is a structured dictionary of terms. In a thesaurus, the terms are arranged so as to display their semantic relationships. Making a thesaurus is dealt with later in this chapter.

Different planning considerations apply to indexes of names of persons, names of corporate bodies, places, and subjects. Combined indexes are common, but the planning decisions cannot be avoided, and should be applied to the name, place or subject components despite their combination in a single alphabetical sequence.

A rule is needed on inversion. An index entry always appears in its alphabetical place, according to the spelling of its first word. The first word must therefore be significant. Often this means that there must be inversion of the natural wording. This is the reason why the military authorities developed their special language for inventories, so much derided in popular talk:

'Seats, lavatory; Officers, for the use of'

The example shows the problem. If the terms are inverted, it ceases to be possible to use the entry in a natural-language context. This may not matter too much with manual indexes, since the users can translate the entries for themselves. It is likely to be a more serious problem with computerized finding aids, because it then becomes difficult to devise a way in which the entry can be printed out in acceptable language: this is a problem of database design.

There is some scope for developing the concept of uniform names and titles: the agreed form of a name which crops up in different contexts, or in different cases. Uniform names are essential in a library context where a single library might find that it holds more than one copy (each perhaps from a different revision) of a book, or more than one title attributed to a single author. Using the uniform name ensures that the items are automatically brought together in a search of the catalogue: it is an illustration of how vocabulary control works through the use of authorities.

Archivists have generally not found a need for this type of authority because (a) they do not generally have multiple copies of a single work; and (b) a reasonable degree of consistency is usually possible within a repository. The uniform name really only becomes unavoid-able where there is some kind of data exchange. MAD2 gives some indicators which would guide practitioners in establishing uniform names. Further development of this authority list is necessary.

Personal names

Some authority is always required to guide indexers of personal names. There should be a rule about how to write the name. The problem of inversion arises. Apart from this a good general rule is that the index entry should follow the most generally used form of the name. This is simple to say, but it is extraordinary how complex the variants of people's names are. Titles of nobility, changes on marriage, *noms de plume*, aliases, all cause problems with British names. As soon as the customs of other countries come into consideration, a host of new forms appear: double surnames, patronymics, problems caused by translation or transliteration.

Historical usage is usually the source of some extra problems. Medieval names are subject to special rules. In Britain the legal form of a name between the late Middle Ages and the early 20th century has four elements:

<Christian name(s)>
<Surame> of <Place of origin or domicile>,
<rank or occupation>.

In the case of women, the legal form in the same period would include a statement of her relationship to a male partner or kinsman, or at least a marriage-category such as 'widow' or 'spinster'. This practice has led some archivists to accept a special data field for name/place, which allows them to record the connection but avoids cluttering place-name indexes with personal references.

MAD2 contains some guidelines on these problems, but its authorities are as yet incomplete. A more complete set of authorities can be found in APPM2, but with a North American bias.

Corporate names

The names of impersonal bodies are likely to be particularly prominent in archival listings because the creators of archives are so frequently organizations. These names present additional problems. There is the question of hierarchical level, which reflects the analysis which underlies the determination of levels of arrangement. There has to be a management decision about determining what is to be

```
┌─────────────────────────────────────────────────────────────────┐
│    Borsetshire County Council                                     │
│       Director of Leisure Services                                │
│          Reference & Research Division                            │
│             Archives Department                                   │
│                Fallowfield Area Archives Office                   │
│                   Parish archives                                 │
│                      Ambridge parish archives ...                 │
└─────────────────────────────────────────────────────────────────┘
```

Figure 5.2 Hierarchical relationship of terms

```
┌─────────────────────────────────────────────────────────────────┐
│ Archives Department, Fallowfield Area Archives Office             │
│ Borsetshire County Council, Director of Leisure Services,         │
│   Reference & Research Division, Archives Department,             │
│   Fallowfield Area Archives Office                                │
│ Fallowfield Area Archives Office                                  │
│ Leisure Services (Director of), Reference & Research Division,    │
│   Archives Department, Fallowfield Area Office                    │
│ Reference & Research Division, Archives Department,               │
│   Fallowfield Area Archives Office                                │
└─────────────────────────────────────────────────────────────────┘
```

Figure 5.3 Chain index references

treated as a group. This was discussed in Chapter 3. It was noted that the organizations which originate groups of archives were often themselves components of an hierarchical tree of other organizations. Because an organization is recognized as having been sufficiently autonomous to be the source of an archive group does not imply that it had no relationship of dependence with another set of organizations. Very often there is an elaborate complex of dependencies. By displaying the name of an archive-producing organization in the context of its environment, it is possible to make it act as one level in an overall thesaurus, or classification of institutions and functions. Figure 5.2 shows a small example of this.

The problem here is how much to display in the index. There is a convention that index entries may be chained, that is, they may show the hierarchical relationships which lie above the term which is the main index entry, but not those which lie below. Thus, there might be alphabetically arranged entries as in Figure 5.2.

An index entry referring to the Fallowfield entry, which occurs in the middle of the hierarchical table, could have the references shown in Figure 5.3.

Within the Fallowfield Area Archives Office there might be no need to spread the net so wide as this, but in a regional or national system, it would probably be necessary to display these rather cumbersome

134

linkages. It might also be necessary to display them as access points in archival descriptions.

Place names

The minimum authority is probably agreement on spelling. Archive services tend to have an official list of names of places within their territorial area of operations (where this is relevant). Once again, there are possible hierarchical orders, which may rank hamlets or townships within historical parishes, for example. Outside the local area, usage should follow a general authority.

Subjects

One problem which belongs to subject indexes is the degree of specificity to be adopted in writing headings. All subject terms belong in a semantic hierarchy (which can be expressed in a thesaurus), and most have multiple facets which can have different meanings in different contexts. Subject references in the text of a document also tend to link together a number of terms.

> The correspondence of Dr Malins, 1831–9, contains references to: medical practice, midwifery, purchase and sale of practices, medical training, the establishment of a general infirmary and a school of medicine.

Figure 5.4 Example of subject terms in a description

Index headings could be chosen from some of these terms, taken in isolation, for example 'midwifery'. Most of them can only be understood if some context can be given: midwifery in general practice in a provincial city in the early 19th century is really the full idea contained in the description. An entry like this, with three qualifiers, is unpractical. A general compromise is to allow two or three qualifiers if they can be expressed in simple phrases. In this example,

> General practice
> Midwifery
> in Birmingham

There are really two kinds of subject index:

1 precoordinate. In these, all the terms involved are brought

135

together into compound entries – they are coordinated first, before the user makes the indicated access. Entries in a precoordinate index are always complex. Typically, each entry contains two or three concepts, resulting in a very specific statement.

Example
Multi-level rule, of archival description, in records management ... [ref.].

This statement has three parts:

(Multi-level rule)
(Archival description)
(Records management)

The parts are linked by logical connectors (in this case 'of' and 'in'). Each part can be unpacked into more extensive statements, each of which suggests additional access points:

Levels of arrangement
Rules of archival description
Description of archives/records
Management of records

These compound statements and the vocabulary they use can be brought together in a thesaurus.

Using an index like this, users can look for an entry which corresponds as closely as possible to the enquiry they have in progress. The problems are (i) that the index will quickly become unwieldy, with its sequences of lengthy entries; and (ii) since the entries have been written by someone translating the terminology of the finding aids, rather than by someone translating the users' requests, there is likely to be more or less of a poor fit between these.

2 postcoordinate. This type of index contains entries which are confined to simple terms. The user has to coordinate these terms after identifying them in the index. Complex statements in the finding aids are therefore likely to generate several index entries.

Example
Rule
Level
Arrangement, etc.

The example shows clearly enough that an index like this rapidly picks up multiple document references. Users who find themselves faced with a dense paragraph of such references, quickly lose interest. Automation can make the thing easier by allowing users to combine terms with 'and', 'or', 'not' operators, but it is essentially an unsatisfactory approach, which will only work in limited situations.

Compromise versions between these two indexing types are possible and normal.

Creating an index

From a practical point of view the main ways of making indexes are the following:

(a) using the facilities of an automated system to create the index (e.g. the facilities of a word processor);
(b) tagging keywords in the text;
(c) putting keywords into dedicated fields;
(d) creating a machine-generated index.

Combinations of these methods are of course possible, but all methods depend on effective vocabulary control, and consistency over time.

Intermediate assistance with vocabulary control can be offered by some software packages, such as word processors or database management systems. In these, it is sometimes possible to link strings of keywords or expressions together, so that searches for one keyword can be answered by reference to others in the same string.

Using the facilities of an automated system

The best example of this is using a word processor. Modern word processors have both text-searching and indexing facilities. Since most typing work is now done by means of word processors, the built-in facilities are probably the simplest and most direct way of creating an index to go with other output. Similar facilities may be offered by other software, or even by operating systems.

Turning on the indexing utility faces the archivist with some instant vocabulary problems. Some of the terms needed for the index appear in the text directly as required for the index, others do not appear in the text, or not in an indexable form. The system therefore has to provide for two alternatives: tagging keywords in the text, and creating separate entries.

In 1596 an ƀAugustinian conventƀ was established at ƀMombasaƀ by Francisco da Gama ... The objects of this mission were twofold, namely, to minister to the spiritual wants of the Portuguese and converts to Christianity along the East African coast, and also to gather others into the fold.[4]

.ix da Gama, Francisco
.ix missionary efforts
.ix Christianity, conversion to

Notes:
Directly usable keywords are tagged 'ƀ'
Additional index entries follow the text and are marked '.ix'

Figure 5.5 Indexing through a word processor

The software is able to extract the marked terms, arrange them alphabetically and attach page or section references.

This simple – perhaps crude – method of indexing a text combines the computer's power to organize textual material with the (trained) human's ability to choose keywords intelligently. A simple authority list can be compiled from the aggregation of terms which the system will produce when the index program is run. Such facilities have saved many thousands of man-hours in making short indexes which relate to word-processed documents; but they are essentially tools worked by human operators. The resulting file of index terms will certainly require more human intervention, in the form of editing to ensure consistency.

Tagging keywords in the text

Most word processors will also search for strings of characters in free text, but lack the full powers of a text-retrieval system.

This limited search utility may be useful where large bodies of text are being processed for inclusion in an automated finding aids system. There are still likely to be problems of consistency in language. Free-text descriptions can be edited, by a skilled human operator, to ensure either that there is a strict conformity to agreed terms, or that the text contains suitable extensions or alternative wording. To use this method effectively, the system should have a synonym facility, and should be able to construct an inverted file.

Putting keywords into dedicated fields

Another alternative is to provide special fields into which terms can be written. This is an approach common in bibliographic description, and is built into data structures like MARC (discussed in Chapter 6). Although in a sense this approach is not consonant with traditional archival description, because it can be seen as an alternative to the writing of free-text fields, the two can easily be combined. It is most useful where there are established authority files, from which the terms entered can be chosen.

Letters of Sister Beatrice, founder, 1810-1860
    Branches, foundation of
    Trixborough
    Parsons, Jane

Figure 5.6 Terms written to dedicated fields

In the world of librarianship, entries such as these are called 'added entries' or 'subject added entries'. (The distinction between these two categories is not one that is useful to the archival community. In library practice, added entries are references to persons, etc., associated with the creation of the original, and subject added entries refer to persons, etc., mentioned in the text. Archivists generally prefer to avoid this distinction, and also make much more use of terms referring to the content of materials than librarians do. Names associated with the creation of archives should be recorded in the administrative history area.) In MAD2, the abstract sub-area is particularly suitable for division into keyword subfields as an alternative to free text, or as an addition to it. MARC AMC has access point fields with tags numbered 6xx and 7xx.

A particular advantage from using a system like this would be the possibility of printing out handlists, that is, sets of descriptions bearing upon a single subject, or based upon a single type of record.

Creating a machine-generated index

The three methods indicated above are ways of combining human and computer power. The selection of index terms is left to human decision, and the computer's contribution is to sort them and allocate the reference numbers to each. The question may arise: is it possible to extend the computer's role?

It would be very desirable if the computer's power could be applied to creating indexes as successfully as it can to providing online access. The trouble is, of course, that the selection of index

139

terms is something that demands intelligence, a knowledge of syntax and an understanding of the meaning of the text which is being treated. Unless there is unforeseen progress with artificial intelligence, it is unlikely that any computer will be able to achieve this in the near future.

However, computers can recognize words or character strings within a text, and can find and sort these quickly and reliably. One possible approach, therefore, is to set up a system which indexes every word. The result of this can be made less unwieldy by including a stop list, thus preventing common words from being included. The intelligibility of the result can be further improved by providing some of the context of each term. The resulting index is of the type known as KWIC (Keyword In Context). The sorted index terms run down the centre of the page, and the remainder of the text they appear in is arranged on the same line, together with the document reference. This type of index can be very effective, though bulky. It is probably most useful when it is applied to a list of titles, where one can be relatively sure that each line of text (being a title) contains a significant brief description.

A variant of the KWIC index is the Keyword Out of Context (KWOC) index, in which the keyword is placed on the left margin and the rest of its contextual line displayed indented below it. This is essentially the same technique. All that the system does is print out the words which have not been stopped, and attach their immediate context and a page number. The real problems have been side-stepped: there is no attempt to solve the problem of selecting

1			Babar's anniversary album: 6 favourite stories	1
2	/	and culture in the	barbarians West: sixth through eighth centuries	
3	/	al work of Charles	Babbage	
4	/	letter to Charles	Babbage, Esq., in reply to his 'Thoughts on the pr	
5		---------Charles	Babbage: pioneer of the computer----------	
6	/		Babbage's Calculating engines: being a collection	1
7			Babbitt	3
8			Babbitt: Roman	1
9		Milton	Babbitt: string quartet no. 2	
10		---------------	Babble-------------------------------	1
11	/	A	babble of ancestral voices: Shakespeare, Cervantes	1
12	/	bo-taal: van socio-	babble tot yuppie-speak	
13	/	A most wondrous	babble: American art composers, their music and th	
14	/		Babcock and Wilcox Limited and Herbert Morris Limi	1

Figure 5.7 Example of KWIC index

Babbage, Charles	
Letter to, in reply to his 'Thoughts...'	[Ref.]
Mathematical work of	[Ref.]

Figure 5.8 Example of a KWOC index entry

keywords, since virtually all words are indexed. There is no attempt to analyse syntax, since all words in the immediate vicinity are displayed. The penalty, of course, is that these indexes are very bulky, and, since there is no vocabulary control, keywords can be found at all points in the alphabet.

Although they are often very useful, KWIC and KWOC indexes now have a decidedly old-fashioned look. They are in regular daily use in library catalogues and for such publications as abstracting journals, which contain highly condensed text and need to be processed very rapidly. Their quaintness comes from their simplicity. Work which still continues on the design of machine-generated indexes makes use of linguistic analysis, and tries to take account of the effects of syntax and context on meaning. Despite some experiments, for example with PRECIS, no currently available indexing system has proved itself in archival circles.[5]

The use of authority files

The discussion so far has highlighted some of the reasons why a fairly comprehensive control of vocabulary terms should be a serious aim. This aspect of authority work should probably be taken up at an early stage in planning for intellectual control. Chief among the authority files needed are lists of names and subject terms. Names of persons and places are generally easier, and most people deal with them first.

Both names and subject terms have hierarchical relationships, but those for names are usually simpler. The authority list will display them. In the case of place names, the hierarchy may be:

(County) [assumed within the county]
  Parish
    Township ...

The problems of relationships of personal names are not so much due to hierarchy as to the fact that people have often had alternative designations. The list will contain all the known alternatives and extensions, and give a reference to the preferred term. In Britain, the

141

main cause of complication is titles of nobility. References to offices held are also needed, since a document may refer to a person by the title of the office being exercised: 'the doctor came to see me yesterday' may refer to a famous surgeon.

The main difficulty is usually in organizing subject terms. It is a matter of debate as to whether archival descriptions can be properly served by accepting an established (i.e. a library-based) subject headings list or not. The discussion, mainly conducted in America, has ranged over several aspects, such as how one might decide what archival materials are 'about'; what other search factors might be used (names and functions in administrative histories; provenance; form, type or genre of materials).

An important reason why library-based subject headings lists are difficult to accommodate to archival descriptions is that they aim to describe the institutions and preoccupations of the present day. Archives necessarily depict situations which existed in the past, even though sometimes the very recent past. Archival descriptions must therefore be able to use the institutional titles and vocabulary which were current at the time when the materials were current.

Subject headings lists are an example of efforts to classify all knowledge. Since a good deal of work has gone into organizing the terms into semantic relationships, it is sometimes useful to cement those relationships by adding a system of codes, or notation, which will act as a shorthand and demonstrate degrees of dependence. The Society of Archivists' scheme did use a notation of this kind. It was perhaps a mistake and was a contributory factor in the abandonment of the scheme, because it seemed such an unnecessary extra difficulty, and because most notation schemes have built-in restrictions. In that shown in Figure 5.9, for example, only ten subcategories are possible in any section.

```
General category 1 – Community Life
        1.3     Regulation and control
                1.31   National Government
                1.33   Local Government
                       1.331  District
                       1.332  City, Borough etc.
```

Source: *Social history and industrial classification*, 1983.

Figure 5.9 Extract from annotated terms list

However, there is no compulsion to use notations in a subject term list, and many systems today do not do so.

Archivists who participate in electronic databases in North America usually have to use the *Library of Congress subject headings*. There is no exact equivalent in Britain, and, as far as is known, no archivist has tried to use one. A distinguishing characteristic of these authorities is that, like library classification schemes, they attempt to classify all knowledge. The advantage of this is that they can be useful in categorizing data from disparate sources and of different kinds. The disadvantage of them is that users have to adapt their descriptions to the pre-existing terms, usually with some difficulty.

Thesauri, on the other hand, normally cover only specialized areas of knowledge. They are built up from actual practice in reading the material, and not from abstract theorizing. Making and using thesauri should form part of the training of every professional in an information profession. It is not difficult, and to make a useful thesaurus is a rewarding experience.

The first step is to draw up a simple list of terms encountered during the ordinary course of work. A start can be made by circulating this list among the archival team, with a note that these terms are to be preferred to any synonym. As work proceeds, new terms are added, and possibly amendments made. Members of the team can be encouraged to send in suggested additions or alterations. A rapid second step is to introduce cross-references, and to indicate which of two or more related terms is to be used.

Work can continue by collecting actual terms met with in the course of descriptive work. The collection and collation process can be illustrated by a flow chart as in Figure 5.10.

It will be seen from this that thesauri always have the advantage of having been compiled empirically from data actually in use, and not from an abstract categorization of knowledge. Additions and alterations are made, not on logical grounds, but as a result of encountering terms during the course of descriptive work.

The final complete thesaurus is a full list of terms applicable to a certain field of activity, in which each term is placed within its semantic context. When it reaches this stage, a thesaurus always has two lists:

• An hierarchically ordered list of terms arranged in their logical relationships

- An alphabetical list (index) of all terms.

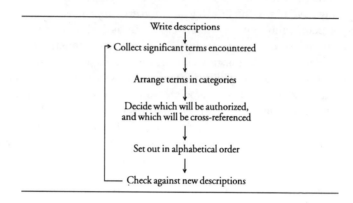

Figure 5.10 The process of making a thesaurus

In expressing the relationship between terms, the following symbols are generally understood:

BT = Broader Term. Gives the term which appears one step further up the hierarchical list

NT = Narrower Term. Gives the term appearing one step below in the hierarchical list

RT = Related Term. Gives terms at the same level of the list

UF Use For. Indicates that this is the approved term for a subject, but points to possible homonyms

USE = Indicates the term to be used where there are alternatives (these must reciprocate with UF terms)

TT = Top Term. Gives the term at the head of the hierarchical tree in which the entry stands

SA = See Also. Gives alternative access points which are allowed by the authority control because of different meaning tracks.

The Top Term allows explanation of which tree of meaning the term being dealt with occurs. This can be useful, because index terms commonly have more than one facet: that is, they can exist in more than one field of action. For example, a school occurs as a level in an hierarchical analysis of education, but also in local government, child

144

```
Education
        Primary education
                Local education authorities
                        Primary schools
                                Barwick County Primary School
        Local administration
                Counties
                        Parishes
                                Parish schools
                                        Barwick C.P. School
        Children
                Day care
                        Schools, etc.
        Architecture
                Public buildings
                        Schools, etc.
        Health
                Preventative medicine
                        School services, etc.
```

Figure 5.11 Facets in which a school name might be relevant

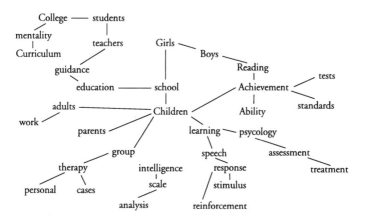

Source: Based on Doyle's association map
Figure 5.12 Association chart

care, architecture, health, and no doubt in other aspects of life. It will have as many places in a table of headings as there are relevant facets.

The ramifications of these facets and the almost endless possibilities of semantic association can be demonstrated by using an *arrow chart*, or *concept association map*.[6]

It should be added that a practical home-made thesaurus does not have to develop these semantic chains. They are useful to indicate possible retrieval approaches, and may be necessary to help control a thesaurus that has got rather large. They are of course a necessary part of a subject headings list or classification scheme.

Thesauri are often home-made, and usually refer to a specialized section of human operations. There is no general thesaurus available for any group of archivists at present. Because there is clearly a need for such a thing, some archivists are adapting the National Register of Archives (NRA) Subject-Index Schema of 1969, and some are using the larger Subject Index Classification which was drafted but never completed by a working party of the Society of Archivists in the mid-1970s. Either of these could be developed into a more generally useful tool for information retrieval within an archives service, or to support data exchange.

Some practical applications of computerized indexing

One of the earliest IT applications to be taken up by some record offices was the possibility of constructing indexes directly usable by readers. This option was attractive because it did not involve redesigning the finding aids (merely giving a new emphasis to a traditional type), and because it promised to help satisfy the very large numbers of readers engaged in family history enquiries.

A well-established and practical example of this approach to technology is that of the Clwyd Record Office, which has two centres, at Hawarden and Ruthin. Using standard software which was available in the employing county's system, they translated their pre-existing indexes into machine-readable form. This had an immediate payoff, since they were able at an early stage to develop online services through the county library network, and to provide users with customized printouts giving lists of local or subject-choice materials. The information given in this way did not include the information held in the central holdings of the repository, but did cover a wide range of peripheral materials, including photographs, printed ephemera, small groups and secondary sources. Even with this limitation, the service was immediately seen as valuable by the existing user groups, and led quickly to the development of new users, especially at a distance.

The Clwyd example shows that a useful service can quickly be built out of peripherals, but also points to the possibility of extending it into the exploitation of the more central holdings. Two points should be noted: (a) the index was placed in the context of a wide-area network at an early stage; (b) the lack of an adequate authority system became obvious at an early stage. It might also be noted that in this archives service the role of indexing was always relatively prominent.

An early and popular choice for computerized indexes was as a means of access to wills. There are examples of this application at the county record offices of Hampshire, Greater London, Leicestershire, and West Sussex. This use of computers is popular with manuscript departments of major libraries, including the British Library and the National Library of Scotland, and it is likely to expand. The ability of a computer to sort keywords into alphabetical order, and to add references, was one which was spotted early. Not much attention has been paid, outside particular schemes, to problems of standardization of vocabulary, and as the indexes increase in bulk, this may present difficulties for users which are not obvious at present.

Of all British archival institutions the National Register of Archives was the most committed to the development of technically competent indexes, and efforts were made over at least two decades to complete this work. The indexing schema published in 1969 became obsolete in the NRA itself fairly rapidly, although it continued in use in a number of record offices. It was followed by pragmatic indexing methods using offline access to a remote computer. Finally towards the end of 1989 a more organized indexing scheme with direct access was mounted. The NRA scheme marks the re-emergence of the index as an important archival tool, on a national level.

Theory and practice of online searching

A few archivists saw the possibilities of interactive searching of computer texts in the early days of computerization. The potential has not yet been realized, at least outside North America. This is in part because of the slow arrival of full-text retrieval systems, but also because archivists perceive that there are serious problems of user education. Before dealing with these, some description of the techniques involved in online searching should be attempted.

To search a computer-held text for specific items within means that there must first be a searcher with the ability to formulate a precise question. A second requirement is that the database which is being searched should contain the appropriate information, and a third requirement is that the computer should be using a system which will manipulate the search request and produce a sensible result. These three elements can be displayed in a diagram.

Searcher: search formulation

↓

System:	top end: verbalization
	....interface
	bottom end: inverted files

Text in database ↑

Figure 5.13 The dynamics of online searching

Formulating sensible questions is a skill which comes with training and practice. It probably demands some knowledge (at least) of the content and structure of the database to be searched. Both of these should be available to the archivists in the repository.

The search request is formulated by selecting one or more keywords which are to be searched for, and linking these by logical operators. This process is often referred to as 'Boolean algebra', in honour of the 19th-century mathematician who first defined these relationships.

Different software systems have different symbols and conventions for searching. The pattern of commands and operators set up in any such system is generally termed the 'command language'. Some are very elaborate and refined, some are simple and crude. Agreement on the standard terms and the way they can be combined is increasingly common, but archivists should avoid software systems which do not have the most common ones, listed below. They should probably also avoid software systems which unduly limit those parts of a database which can be searched interactively.

In an archival context, it is only necessary to know the following:

148

1 Boolean operators: AND, OR, NOT

AND asks the system to find cases where each of the terms specified occur in the same document. It excludes documents which contain one or more but not all of the specified terms. It is important to be aware of the different effect of this command, and commands using 'OR'.

OR asks for cases where *one* of the specified terms occurs in a document, and therefore produces all documents which refer to any one of them.

NOT is used to exclude a term or a category. It seeks to produce all cases where the specified term is not present.

2 Positional operators: SAME, ADJACENT, NEAR (these commands vary from system to system)

[Term] SAME [Term] asks for cases where the two terms specified occur in the same field or section of the text.

ADJ[acent] asks for cases where the two terms occur next to each other.

NEAR brings up cases where they occur near to each other. The system may allow them to be in a different order, and may have facilities for specifying exactly how near to each other they should be, e.g. within five words.

3 Value operators: = =>, =< ,<, >, LIKE, CONTAINS

These terms control the way the system matches the search term with the data. Equal to (=) means that the search term must exactly match the target. Greater or less than (>, <) probably applies most often to numerical data, but some systems can apply it to literal characters. In these cases, 'w' is less than 's'. [Term] LIKE [Term] asks for cases where there is a resemblance, e.g.:

Searcher: Title LIKE 'ogre'
Computer response: Pro*gre*ss reports
                     Work in pro*gre*ss
                     The den of the *Ogre*s

CONTAINS has a similar effect, but may operate where a smaller amount within a larger, or a phrase within a paragraph, is specified.

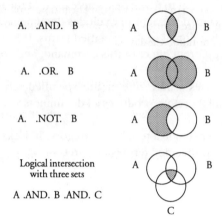

[Shaded areas indicate hits]

A. .AND. B   A   B

A. .OR. B   A   B

A. .NOT. B   A   B

Logical intersection
with three sets   A   B

A .AND. B .AND. C

C

Figure 5.14 Venn diagram to illustrate retrieval commands

4 One mathematical convention for their use, the bracketing of complex terms

There are additional Boolean and other operators, and facilities proper to particular systems.

It is traditional to explain the use of the logical operators by using a Venn diagram.[7] From this it can be seen that there are four typical cases.

Some of the problems of searching databases can be illustrated by a practice search. In the following example, it is assumed that the database contains descriptions of local archive materials.

Searchers might begin by searching on a single term. For example:

Search request: Jones
Computer response: There were 16 occurrences of this term in 8 documents.

The 16 hits in 8 documents then form the 'hit file' or, in more formal language, the 'retrieved list'. Further searching can then be concentrated on this restricted set of documents.

Difficulties arise if the name in the search request is not exactly the same as the name in the database. For example, when searching for a place name, historical spellings (or even misspellings) may often be present. There are two ways in which this difficulty can be partially met.

Firstly, the system may offer help. It should permit 'fuzzy' searches, where only the core strings of characters are asked for; for example (the database contains 'Calday'):

Searcher:	Caldey	
Computer response:	No documents satisfy this condition	
Searcher:	Cald$	
Computer response:	Calday	1 occurrence
	Calderton	1 occurrence

Alternatively, the system may give access to the internal index, or inverted file:

Searcher:	Show dictionary at C
Computer response:	Calday
	Calderton

Since most retrieval systems do work by constructing an internal concordance or dictionary, containing all the words in the searchable part of the text (except common words excluded by a 'stop list'), it is useful if searchers can have access to this list of terms.

The other way is by constructing appropriate dictionaries externally, for use as authorities within the system. A local archives service, for example, will probably find it useful to compile a list of local names, arranged perhaps in an hierarchical table by parish or township. A searcher who fails to find 'Calday' might pick up appropriate references from 'West Kirby', the name of the ancient parish in which the place is situated. This illustrates one example of the problems that archivists encounter because they work with historical materials.

Database searching by simple terms can sometimes be helped forward by limiting the field of search. The effectiveness of this strategy depends much on the design of the database. For example:

Searcher:	Calday at Text

This command, using the language of the particular system in force, means that the search for the term 'Calday' should be confined to the data held within the field called 'Text'. The main advantage offered by this limitation would be that it saves computer effort. If the database is very large, this may save a significant amount of time; but the searcher would have to be sure that all the relevant hits would in fact be within the Text field.

However, there are other possibilities. The database might have been designed so that certain types of data have been written into fields dedicated to them. These are often termed *valued fields*. They could be used to contain terms which are very specific or technical. Examples are: reference codes, type/quantity of material, first and last dates, location codes.

Searcher: At_Firstdate = >1845

This command would ask the computer to produce all records in which the entry in the field 'Firstdate' was equal to or greater than 1845. The symbol '@' is commonly used for 'At'.

Searcher: 'QS/16/188' at Refcode

This command would produce the one document whose reference code was the one quoted. (Note that most computer systems ask users to enclose characters which appear in the text within single quotation marks, so that the system can differentiate them from characters which are part of commands.)

So far, the examples have shown how searchers may examine the contents of a database by specifying simple search terms. The next step is to offer multiple or complex terms, so as to direct the search more accurately at the final target.

The simplest case of a complex search term is where there is more than one word used to express a single object or concept. For example:

Searcher: Parish registers

Many computer systems would read this request as meaning that there were two search terms, 'parish' and 'register', linked by the default Boolean operator OR. These systems would therefore look for documents containing either of the terms. This search might therefore succeed, but might also produce a result such as:

Computer response: Aintree hospital registers
                                   Walton parish accounts
                                   St Nicholas nominal payment registers

In this example, the searcher should have entered a command like one of the following:

Searcher:	Parish AND registers
	Parish NEAR registers

The first of these would produce all cases in which the term 'parish' occurred in the same record as the term 'registers' (note that the plural is significant in this example: in real life 'register' or 'register$' would be used). Some unwanted entries might appear, but the hit file should certainly include all cases where the data use the phrase 'parish registers'.

The second case would bring up all cases where the two terms occurred within a stated space of each other. (Many systems allow the searcher to specify how far apart the terms might be, for example within six words). It might therefore find the record which includes the phrase 'registers of St Nicholas parish', which otherwise might be lost owing to incorrect wording.

Uncontrolled vocabulary still has its dangers, however, as for example 'church registers' would not be found, nor would any case where the word 'parish' was omitted. 'Burial registers' would not be found by the search in the last example.

Searcher:	Parish ADJ [adjacent to] register

This command would certainly find all cases in which 'parish register' appeared in the text of the database, and would not retrieve any variation; but it would miss cases where the wording was not authorized, such as 'St Nicholas registers'.

The next step is to combine two or more search terms, whether they are simple or complex.

Searcher:	Burial$ ADJ register$ NOT parish AND Kirkby

Here the request is for all cases in which the term 'burial/s' occurs next to the term 'register/s' where the parish of Kirkby is excluded. The searcher is looking for all burial registers except those of Kirkby. Systems generally do their calculations from left to right, so in effect this statement will be treated as follows:

Burial$ ADJ (register$ NOT parish) AND Kirkby

The effect of the brackets is to cause the system to calculate the formula within them before continuing with the rest of the command.

In all probability, what the searcher had intended was:

Burial$ ADJ register$ NOT (parish AND Kirkby)

The difference between these two might not have been significant in this case. Whether it was or not depends on the field structure and content of the database being searched. In general the presence and order of bracketed compound terms makes an important difference; it may mean the difference between success and failure in any particular search.

Any number of bracketed terms may be used, and they may be nested within other brackets. For example:

Searcher: At_<date 1800 AND burial$ ADJ register$ NOT parish AND Kirkby

This command seeks to find all cases where there are burial/s register/s earlier in date than 1800 in all parishes except Kirkby. It might be better expressed as:

((Burial$ ADJ register$) NOT (parish AND Kirkby)) AND
At_date 1800

In practice, it is nearly always better to use simple searches and refine the question in a sequence of requests:

Searcher: Burial$ ADJ register$
Computer response: 120 documents satisfy the conditions
Searcher: Parish NOT Kirkby
Computer response: 82 documents satisfy the conditions
Searcher: At_date <1800
Computer response: 12 documents satisfy the conditions
Searcher: Display all

Conventions have grown up which control the way in which search terms are presented to the computer. Generically these conventions are called 'command languages', and are specific to each software system. Some features of the many command languages are now becoming standard over much of the industry. For example, there are signs that the command language known as SQL (Structured Query Language) is transcending the boundaries of the single proprietary system where it originated, and is becoming standard. In SQL, search requests are expressed nearly in natural language, but in a set order, e.g.:
Select <field names>
from <database name>

where <variable>=<value> [elaborated as a search formula]
order by <specified order>.

Putting together a search formulation which conforms to this is a skill which could be learned by any reasonable person. However, there are pitfalls. For example, field names specified must be present in the database, and must be spelt correctly; the sequence of search terms must be correct, including the use of ' ' to indicate non-numerical quoted text, and so forth. Because of these complications, search request formulations must be regarded as technically skilled operations, outside the scope of most lay people.

Systems are now appearing which will reduce the technicality of search requests, and allow them to be input in completely natural language.

Example

What do we know about new building in rural townships during the 18th century, in cases where there was high population growth?

The system converts this internally into an SQL sequence, and applies it to the database. As always the value of the result depends primarily on the aptness, accuracy and completeness of the data held in the file. No practical system using this technology is available to small or intermediate archives services at the time of writing.

The problem of the interface with unskilled users is also being approached by the development of expert systems. These are elaborate sets of computer programs in which the rules of work operation are loaded into memory, together with the necessary data. Using these, advanced computers are able to guide users along an enquiry path, giving them a sequence of questions and narrowing down the search on the basis of the answers. These systems are at an experimental stage.[8]

Notes and references

1 Published in the *Society of Archivists newsletter*, **60**, Mar. 1992.
2 *MAD2*, 8.4B.
3 Black, Elizabeth, *Authority control: a manual for archivists*, Planning Committee on Descriptive Standards, Bureau of Canadian Archivists, Ottawa, 1991.
4 Gray, J., *History of Zanzibar*, Oxford University Press, 1962, 45. The tagging convention shown follows Word*Star usage.

5 Experiments at the PRO and at the Devon Record Office: *Journal of the Society of Archivists*, **6**, 1978, 116-17.
6 Doyle, L.B., 'Indexing and abstracting by association', *American Documentation*, **13**, 1962, 378-90. Some computer systems operate by noting the verbal associations and measuring the strength of the relationship indicated statistically.
7 Davis, C. H., and Rush, J. E., *Guide to information science*, Library Association, London, 1979, 70.
8 Michelson, Avra, *Expert systems technology and its implications for archives*, National Archives Technical Information Paper No.9, National Archives and Records Administration, Washington, DC, Mar. 1991.

6

Data exchange

The uses of archival description

In Chapter 4 the processes involved in creating a finding aids system were discussed, and some of the needs of users were considered insofar as they affected the design of that system. The present chapter continues by examining some of the uses to which finding aids can be put.

The theory of archival description is that it aims to create representations of the originals, in order to carry out a variety of purposes. Some of these purposes are connected with the internal administration of the repository. Others are to provide a service to users. All user-oriented finding aids have one basic aim: they are intended to help users to identify the archival entities which they need, or might need, to retrieve for examination. There is a general presumption that users will need to retrieve the original materials for their reference needs, but some finding aids are so effective as representations that they can also be used to supply information for which users would have searched the originals. So, while most finding aids are primarily intended to be used within the repository, some are also suitable for facilitating the use of archival materials at a distance.

The range of possible uses for finding aids is wide. At one end of it, a finding aid might simply inform users that an entity exists, and has certain characteristics (e.g. that a class is large or small, and covers particular date ranges). A finding aid like this can be useful at a distance. The annual publication *Accessions to repositories* is based upon this observation.[1] A brief listing of this kind can also be useful in reconstituting scattered groups.

The descriptions which appear as components of a national information system are further on in the same range of types. The

American *National union catalog of manuscript collections* (NUCMC) is an example. It contains summaries of the content of the groups mentioned in it. These may be extensive enough to provide initial access points for the users of original materials.

At the far end of the range of types of finding aid, description is so complete that there is surrogation: users can rely on the finding aid for most of the information held in the original, which they may not actually need to see. This kind of description merges, of course, into the publication of edited texts. It has always been a recognized area of work with primary materials. Although the pressure of work, the growth in quantity of archives, and the increase in range of users' interests have reduced the relative importance of this kind of publication, it is still actively pursued in many places, and even shows signs of revival.

All the descriptions mentioned so far can be produced in traditional formats by manual methods. The coming of computers has increased the range of possibilities by presenting archivists with the idea of the shared database. Such databases are now common in the library world, and elsewhere. It would be strange if this possibility were not to cause changes in archival management.

The two extreme cases mentioned above correspond broadly to two kinds of database: bibliographic and full-text. Historically, the production of full-text or calendar-type representations was anterior to inventory-type representations. In the period before the foundation of permanently administered archival systems, the publication of texts was regarded as the prime duty of archivists, and this tradition lingered for a very long time.[2] Jenkinson's classic textbook of archival management assumed that if there was any time left from the prime duty of archivists, which was preservation, then it should be directed to preparing editions of original texts.[3] Originally, therefore, it was assumed that the transmission of data and texts was central to the purpose of an archives service, or at least came second only to basic preservation.

As a matter of general principle, finding aids are in the public domain (even where the originals they refer to may be closed), and are made available through appropriate media. Some finding aids have therefore always been seen as facilitating remote use. These are the ones which have been formally published, or which are intended for dissemination to other repositories or reference centres, or for exchange with other finding aids from such places.

In this way it can be seen that archival descriptions have two characteristics which their originals do not have:

1 They can be distributed to points remote from the repository which are convenient for some user groups.
2 They can be organized internally, or given a special apparatus of retrieval aids, in ways which will significantly add to the ability of users to extract information from them.

These characteristics have always existed implicitly. As far back in history as there has been systematic exploitation of archival materials, there has been a tradition of the distribution of finding aids (or at least of archival representations). Collectors, librarians and archivists have published, distributed or exchanged sets of archival descriptions. Major libraries have shared in this tradition by publishing their own catalogues of holdings, and calendars of documents, and have collected similar materials issued by other libraries. The Royal Commission on Historical Manuscripts (HMC) began its programme of publication of transcripts and abstracts soon after 1869, and was itself simply continuing an earlier tradition.[4]

The foundation of the National Register of Archives in 1945 formalized a previous tradition, up to then rather haphazard, of exchanging, collecting and centralizing finding aids. The NRA made itself a central exchange point of archival descriptions, and actively duplicated and distributed lists as well as collecting them to build up a central reference facility. Getting the appropriate descriptions to the user groups identified as needing them is a constant in archive administration. So is the tendency of archivists to join groups of their users as fellow-workers in a particular research enterprise.

The finding aids so distributed and exchanged have customarily included retrieval aids as well as descriptions. The paging and layout of published material has always received attention, and retrieval aids have included chapter and page headings, explanatory glosses and notes. Most importantly, the provision of an index has always been thought an essential feature of a published finding aid. Sometimes an index has been important enough to be the main part of a publication.[5]

It has also been customary to use the technology currently available to facilitate the distribution and exchange of archival descriptions. Printing texts and abstracts began almost as soon as printing technology became common. As printing developed into a cheap and easily available medium, so publishing schemes developed and expanded, culminating in the ambitious projects of the late 19th and early 20th centuries.[6] The invention and elaboration of record type, as a means of reproducing medieval manuscripts, is comparable to the adoption of electronic techniques for publishing primary material for the use of an expert community.

In the present century, microforms appeared as a practical technology, and in the period after the Second World War it became the medium for several important projects in information exchange. Perhaps the most significant of all these schemes, in terms of its long-term effects, was the seizure and publication in microform of series of German government archives after 1945.

On the international scene, further grand schemes followed. Unesco initiated mass microfilming in order to remedy some of the problems of cultural identity in the aftermath of colonial withdrawal, or of boundary changes caused by war. Similar projects were set up by individual countries, such as Australia, Canada, Ghana and Kenya, which found that much of their archival heritage was held in former metropolitan countries. Within Britain large-scale microfilming projects continued into the 1980s. The *National inventory of documentary sources*[7] was launched at this time. This project amounts to an attempt at constructing a national data exchange scheme for archival and some other primary materials, based on microform technology.

The practicality of microforms has always been restricted by the initial processing costs and by the relative difficulty of reading the material. Even so, microfilming projects have exceeded printed publication of archival texts greatly in the amount and range of material covered, even if they have not fully succeeded in attracting broad public interest. There remained a potential for a data exchange scheme using an easier medium. It is not surprising that when computers began to appear as instruments for the communication and exchange of information – in effect as a means of publication – that use began to be made of these too, for archival descriptions. The rest of this chapter concerns the way this has been done, or might be done.

The background to electronic archival data exchange

Naturally enough, the most rapid advance in using computers to exchange archival data has been made in North America. This has been the leading region for technological advance, and an important number of American archivists are employed in large academic institutions where advanced technologies are commonly available. As soon as it appeared that electronic channels offered feasible methods of data exchange, some of these archivists were prepared to experiment, and to raise funds for investment.

The first successful network for carrying archival data was SPINDEX, a cooperative system initially developed in the largest repositories of the USA in the late 1960s. The experiment ran for 20 years, had considerable success and spread quite widely before it was finally wound up as technologically outmoded. It was limited by the capacity of the technology of the time: for example, input had initially to be by punched card or tape, and the system aimed to produce printed copy. It contained provision for printing out indexes, but not for online searching. However, several features were used which have proved important in the design of archival databases, and these should be recognized.

The SPINDEX databases were the first to introduce a formalized set of levels of description for use between repositories, and to make these the basis for data exchange. Each entry was given a reference number which was long enough to include an indication of the level used. Armed with this, archivists could enter descriptions of material at every level, and these could be extracted in proper order and with hierarchical relationships preserved. This feature is necessary if the database is multi-level and is to remain 'clean'.

Secondly, a data structure was provided in SPINDEX which allowed a flexible division of information into variable-length fields, each identified by a numerical tag. These tags looked like MARC tags and used some of the conventions of MARC, but did not actually come from a MARC format.

A third feature of importance was that there were authorities for controlling the production of indexes from the different fields.

In these three ways, SPINDEX showed that American archivists had recognized all the basic problems of cooperative data exchange, and had set up means (including cooperative management) of dealing with them. In these early years there was also a British attempt to establish a computer-based data exchange for archives. This was PROSPEC-SA, which ran experimentally for a year or so in 1977–8. By comparison with SPINDEX, this experimental system was rather more rough-and-ready. It did not have a formal means of recognizing levels

161

of description, had only very basic authority controls and no central apparatus for controlling the structure or use of the database.

Because of the experience they gained with SPINDEX (and with some other systems), American archivists were in a position to go on to develop further infrastructural standards, and this in turn allowed them to participate in the very large data exchange networks which developed in the library world at the end of the 1970s. Chief among these infrastructural authorities was the MARC AMC format, which was completed and published by 1984. With this available, archivists were able to approach the controllers of the main cooperative electronic bibliographic databases, and successfully propose that they should share in the enterprise.

Technical standards for data exchange

The infrastructural standards for data exchange are formulated and maintained by the International Standards Organization (ISO), which is advised by the international professional associations: the International Federation of Library Associations and Institutions (IFLA), the International Federation of Documentalists (FID) and the International Council on Archives (ICA).

Libraries had been able to make progress with the exchange of bibliographic data because after 1977 they had access to an international standard for the structure of these data. In that year, IFLA began publishing the International Standard Bibliographic Description formats (ISBDs). An ISBD version now exists for the description of most of the various materials that libraries have to deal with, including older (antiquarian) books, monographs and non-book materials. The ISBDs are used as authorities controlling the structure of entries in cooperative databases. Without these underlying standards it would have been difficult to establish the electronic formats.

The ISBDs establish what is required for a description from a professional (library) point of view. The standard which is required for database construction from the point of view of the technical electronic format, is laid down by the ISO. Several ISO standards exist which control the technical design of any data exchange system. The many ISO standards cover matters such as the arrangement of bits in an electronic message; the heading protocols needed for the exchange of such messages from one system to another; methods for arranging alphanumeric character strings; international character sets; and the structure of complex textual files.

Most of these standards are necessary preliminaries to the setting up of any database. Archivists must inevitably make use of them, and perhaps should know more about them than they generally do. They should have some familiarity at least with the *Specification for a data descriptive file for information interchange* (ISO 8211).[8] But in general, archivists do not need to understand the technical complexities of such standards, only that they are there and that no data exchange system can be successful without them.

Once the detailed and technical requirements of an electronic database have been established, the question of the format of the information to be held in it can be considered. A technical international standard has been produced to provide a framework on which new electronic databases can be built. This is the Common Communication Format (CCF), produced under the aegis of Unesco. Clearly, it would not be reasonable to embark on the construction of a shared database which did not conform to this basic standard.

More firmly established, and now with a long tradition of use, is MARC (MAchine-readable ReCord). This is a standard format for writing bibliographical descriptions into an electronic medium. It is used as a structure for all data held in library databases, and, although there are national and specialist variations, is international in character. UNIMARC is an international form, and CANMARC and UK MARC are examples of other national variants, used in Canada and Britain respectively.

Each country which has electronic databases in its information system, has a committee or organization which is responsible for maintaining and developing the MARC format used. Because of this, national variations continue to develop, but these are to some extent restrained by the need to communicate internationally, and by the existence of the international standards which accompany the national formats.

Databases using MARC formats are to be found all over the world, and since electronic media are capable of being sent and received everywhere, the format must be regarded as an essential feature of databases which contain descriptions of information-bearing materials ('bibliographic' descriptions).

Archives and Manuscripts Control (AMC) is a variation of the USMARC format which was developed by American archivists and authorized by the Society of American Archivists, as well as by the MARC controlling body for the USA. Although it accepts (of course) the basic structure and style of the general MARC format, AMC provides an adapted structure which allows archival descriptions to be expressed in a suitable way. These descriptions can then be incorporated into an electronic database.

Both of the two largest bibliographic databases operating in North America, the Online Computer Library Center (OCLC) and the Research Libraries Network (RLIN) have adopted a form of the USMARC AMC standard, and now include many thousands of archival descriptions in their data. Although probably most descriptions are of groups ('collections'), descriptions have also been entered of materials at all levels, down to and including items. RLIN has an advisory committee which maintains the AMC standard applicable to it, and deals with questions for decision which come up periodically. Another committee represents archivists' needs to the overall controlling body for the American version of MARC. The largest repositories of the USA, including the Library of Congress and the National Archives and Records Administration (NARA), are now members and users of this network.

The pattern of all MARC variants sets out a sequence of fields, some fixed-length, some variable, which together contain all the bits of data

100	Name of principal creator of the archive or
110	Name of creating body or organization
245	Title statement, with subfields for form/type/genre, the name element, covering dates
300	Physical description: subfields for number and kind of material
351	Description of the arrangement of the entity (for example: arranged in five subgroups – GC (general correspondence); SP (speeches); MI (miscellaneous files), etc.)
545	Administrative history or biographical information
520	Abstract: summary of the contents
541	Immediate source of acquisition
561	Provenance information
773	Linking parent–child relationships between descriptions (e.g. group–class)
600 and 700 series	Access points: names, subjects etc.[9]

Figure 6.1 Principal MARC AMC fields and tags

needed to construct a bibliographic description. The fields are identified by giving each one a numerical tag, which in the main is standard everywhere. Many of the fields are also subdivided, each subfield being labelled by a different tag. Dividing out the data in this way facilitates their exchange and retrieval. The basic design of course reflects the needs of library services.

Those who work with the MARC format rapidly get used to the pattern of fields and the tags that identify them.

The problem which archivists experience with this system is of course that it is a flat file. Each entry is equivalent to each other entry, and proceeds item by item. The AMC variant attempts to overcome this by providing fields in which the linkages between descriptions at different levels can be explained. It is accompanied by rules which guide archivists in the way they should use the various fields, and provides for cataloguing rules and authorities which are suitable for archival descriptions. Nevertheless the basic structure resembles the main MARC format. It expects users to complete fields which represent author/creator; title; summary of content; and strings of 'added entries' (keywords to serve as access points).

At present, the AMC variety of MARC operates only as a variant of USMARC, the form of MARC adopted by the Library of Congress and certain associated bodies. There is no AMC version of any other national MARC version,[10] but USMARC AMC is used by a number of important repositories outside the USA.[11] The format is attractive not only because it allows participation in large bibliographic databases but also because there are purpose-designed software packages available which use it.

Cataloguing standards

The ISBDs are cataloguing standards, although in their basic form they need elaboration into practical rules before they can be used in working libraries. Fully developed rules are needed to complete the framework of necessary infrastructure. There are two kinds of these. Both fall within the professional sphere of interest of archivists: they are professional, rather than technological standards:

- a cataloguing standard aims to control the shape and composition of descriptions
- authority lists or files provide controls over the vocabulary and

165

terminology used in descriptions, and hence over information retrieval from them.

In the library world, the most commonly accepted rules for cataloguing are the *Anglo-American cataloguing rules*, second edition (AACR2). These rules are widely accepted internationally. They include variations for particular types of material, such as graphic materials, maps, microforms, films, music, sound recordings, objects and manuscripts. A variation for machine-readable files is under development.

From an archival point of view, the ISBD standards and AACR2 can be considered together. AACR2 does have a chapter for the cataloguing of manuscripts, and archivists ought to be familiar with this, since it is a standard which is available to colleagues in many parts of the world, more widely distributed and less restricted by cultural boundaries than any archival standard, and because the data structure of AACR2 is closely allied to that of MARC.

AACR2 provides 11 areas, the data elements of which add up to a full bibliographic description. There is a consensus that the AACR2 format is not suitable for archival descriptions because:

(a) the areas correspond to those required by printed books. It is assumed, for example, that each manuscript has a title and an author, and something corresponding to publication data;

(b) there is no recognition in the rules that there are differences of level, and although it is possible to adapt the standard to describe collectivities (such as groups), the resulting set of descriptions is a flat file, each entry being equivalent to all others;

(c) the authorities provided are not the most suitable for archivists or manuscript curators.

The style of an AACR2 description is recognizable at once. The central principle is the separation of data into a number of fields, many of which are (in MAD2 terminology) dedicated: that is, they each contain only one clearly defined piece of data, such as a date, a place of publication, number of pages, etc. There are, of course, variable-length fields which contain descriptive text, but, in the spirit of the AACR2 approach, keywords for information retrieval are placed in dedicated fields outside the main text. This makes it easy to retrieve them, but derives, historically, from the model of a card index. The technical term for these keywords is 'added entries' or 'subject added entries' (generically 'access points'), referring originally to additional cards placed in the main index. This terminology is not directly apt for archival descriptions, although there is no principle of archive administration which would discourage the use of dedicated fields for keywords.

Because these rules appeared first, and because many archivists work in libraries, there have been attempts to adapt AACR2 for archival descriptions. The most important of these is S. Hensen's *Archives, personal papers and manuscripts* (APPM). The second edition of this (APPM2), adopted by the Society of American Archivists and by the controlling bodies of the online databases, was published in 1989. It contains rules for writing an archival 'bibliographic' description, and extensive authority lists. The archival descriptions may be of collectivities, and may contain sections which link together sets of descriptions in an hierarchical order: in other words, it can be used to give multi-level descriptions in conformity with archival practice. The question of the 'authorship' of official archives is also tackled. The authority lists are specially composed in order to answer the special needs of archivists, e.g. for historical names and subject terms.

APPM is a standard which is compatible with AACR2, but which can cope with the special characteristics of archives. Using it, archivists can produce what may be properly (and technically) termed bibliographical descriptions, that is, entries in shared databases or intended for exchange through shared channels. This type of description is not the same as a finding aid in a finding aids system. Indeed, it is assumed by APPM that finding aids will be the main source from which information is obtained for writing bibliographic descriptions. Repositories continue to need finding aids which are more varied and detailed than bibliographic descriptions.

From the first, many archivists exposed to APPM have argued that its closeness to AACR2 made it undesirable as a standard for archival description. The most important alternative which has appeared so far is the Canadian *Rules for archival description* (RAD) which, after much preliminary consultation, began to be published in 1990. RAD accepts certain basic affinities with AACR2, but attempts to base its actual practice on essential archival principles. Both RAD and APPM have numbered rules and paragraphs which correspond closely to related passages in AACR2.

Outside North America, archivists have rarely been closely familiar with library practices, and especially with the highly technical aspects which are evident in AACR2 and in MARC. It is probable that Sweden is the only European country in which archivists have been at all acquainted with MARC fields.[12] Archives services and their staffs, even where they have been part of library administrations, have usually had a separate management system and a separate training and career structure. Consequently there has been no pressure in Europe for an adaptation either of library cataloguing rules or of MARC for archival participation.

The need for standards to underlie the development of electronic data exchange was, however, perceived. In Britain, the need was met by the publication in 1990 of the *Manual of archival description*, second edition (MAD2). This contains rules and guidelines for writing archival finding aids, that is, archival descriptions which are not necessarily bibliographic; they are for use within the repository and not only for data exchange.

MAD2 provides a standard for the construction of finding aids systems, the basic descriptive work done by repositories, whether or not they have any electronic equipment.

MAD2 as it exists at present is almost without authority lists, whereas more than half of APPM2 consists of these. Authorities for archives should include lists of names of individuals and corporate bodies, places, subject terms, and terms for the exact description of types of archive. Generally, it is difficult for archivists to adopt library-based authorities for any of these terms, because of the difficulties caused by historical reference.

To deal with entities which existed in the past, but which are no longer operative or have changed their names or their character over time, additional terms and special conventions are needed. Terms have often changed their meaning. For example, describing the archives of the Poor Law, operative in England from 1601 to 1929, it is necessary to have references to Overseers of the Poor, Guardians, Unions, workhouses, out-relief, etc., and these references should not appear under broader terms which relate primarily to present-day social welfare provision. Similar problems can be found in almost every sphere of human activity. (There is also a possible difficulty in reconciling historical usage with 'politically correct' language.)

It is obvious that authority lists should provide for new vocabulary and for the needs of local and specialist repositories. There is a need for constant maintenance of the authorities, which is usually done by working parties appointed by the professional association concerned. The professional association is also the body most responsible for the initial construction of authority files, and for getting them authorized by the controlling bodies of databases or national information systems.

Using the online databases

The proprietary online databases which contain archival material have two categories of participant. The principal group consists of full members, who are institutions which pay a sustaining subscription to the service, and have the privilege of entering new data, and amending or withdrawing it as necessary. The secondary group consists of institutions and individuals who pay a smaller fee and have the right simply to have a terminal and access the data.

The database RLIN may be taken as a case study. The controlling body is the Research Libraries Group (RLG), based at Stanford University in California. RLG is maintained by a group of research libraries to provide many common services. The RLIN database itself contains several specialized sections, one of which is devoted to archival materials. By early 1990, there were many thousands of entries in this section.

Archival data is entered using MARC AMC and has APPM as a built-in cataloguing standard. Authorities can be called up online by archivists engaged in entering new data. Participating repositories usually compile a list of interpretations and local rules, for the use of their staff when entering data. The most important of these local rules and conventions were published in the SAA's *Compendium of practice*. Technical problems relating to the entry of archival descriptions are also discussed online through the 'Archives and Archivists List', carried by BITNET and INTERNET. British archivists are able to join in this electronic forum, as it is available through JANET.[13]

Archival entries into RLIN are usually derived from rough listings or internal finding aids prepared in the repository; an important proportion of entries are from backlog descriptions, and several repositories have been able to secure grants to enable them to translate accumulations of archival finding aids, inherited from the past, into the new format.

Unlike some other database systems, RLIN works through dedicated terminals, which are used for both input and output. RLIN work in large libraries is usually integrated or closely associated with the library's own online public-access catalogue (OPAC), and many of these catalogues are also available nationally and internationally through networks.

For entering new data, formatted screens appear, the MARC AMC tags appearing at the top and left of the screen. The data for many of the fields are automatically supplied by the system: for example, the date of the entry, the name of the repository, the unique entry number. Defaults can be provided for several other fields, such as the predominant language of the materials being described, or its state of conservation. The variable-length fields are filled by descriptive entries conforming in depth with the in-house rules. This does of course allow a good deal of variation, and overall the database is fairly tolerant of many different styles and modes of operation.

RLIN (but not other similar databases) has an area called the ARC segment, which corresponds broadly to the Management Information Sector of the MAD2 data elements table. This consists of one or more screens of administrative data relating to the processing of the archival materials described. The ARC sector can contain the accessions register, notes of future action, conservation data or information on records management actions at set dates in the future. This part of the record is protected, and cannot be seen by users who are not authorized members of the originating repository staff. Many participants, however, prefer to use their own in-house computer system for this type of information, which does not carry a fee for making or referring to the entry, and which can still be linked with the RLIN record locally. Because of this, many software packages for archival description designed for use in the USA, employ a MARC AMC structure.

Descriptions which are entered into RLIN become available to all users worldwide. These users can access data in a variety of ways, but most usually by means of an online search. The descriptions are broken down into AMC fields, which are either dedicated or free-text. The dedicated fields can be retrieved and sorted, and the free-text fields can be searched. Because of the underlying AACR2 approach to cataloguing (by way of APPM2), some fields contain only index terms, either derived from authority lists or locally generated. These terms can of course be accessed by users, who follow the semantic path set out by the authority control. In the case of RLIN, the authority

Archive	Collier, John, 1884-1968.
MSGR	Papers, 1992-1968
56	75 Linear ft. (150 boxes)

Organization: Correspondence: arranged chronologically.
Summary: Indian rights advocate, teacher, author. John Collier, commissioner of Indian affairs, directed a dramatic shift in federal Indian policy. The records reflect Collier's private thoughts and impact during critical years in Indian social and political history.
Unrestricted access.
Finding aids: Unpublished registry in repository.

1. American Indian Defense Association, Inc.   2. Indians of North America–Government relations–Sources.

0

<Loc.	<1XX> Main entry, <#d> dates
stamp>	<245 #k> Title (form), <#f> inclusive dates.
<RGPN>	<300 #a> Physical extent of item.

<351> Organization and arrangement notes <#3> Material: <#b> arrangement.
<520> Summary notes.
<506> Restrictions on access notes.
<555> Finding aids notes.

1. <6XX> Subject heading.   2. <6XX> Subject heading.

0

Figure 6.2 Example of output from a MARC AMC file (RLIN style)

171

for subject terms is the Library of Congress Subject Headings (LCSH). There is provision for one or more local authority lists in each entry.

Data exchange outside North America

The last decade of the 20th century is characterized by the rapid development of computer networks, online databases and teletext/viewdata services. Outside the USA and Canada approaches by way of library-based interchange systems and the MARC format do not seem to have attracted the interest of archivists, even in countries which have strong national leadership and an interest in the technological development of information services, such as France.

In Britain, the electronic media have been used as a means of publishing quite large amounts of archival data. These projects, based in university repositories, explicitly do not aim at data exchange, but at exploiting the material in historical research and as an educational resource. The means of publication is the Joint Academic Network (JANET), which is an all-purpose electronic link between academic institutions. JANET has gateways to similar academic and communication networks elsewhere, such as the European Academic Network (EARN), BITNET, INTERNET and others. JANET also carries the OPACs of the main academic libraries, and archival descriptions can also appear as undifferentiated access points in some of these.

It is therefore possible to access files, and to exchange messages through JANET to any address which participates in such a network, worldwide. No standard formats are required, only a computer system which links to the network. Consequently, data published by this means can only be accessed and interpreted by using standards and controls adopted by each creating agency.

Southampton University used the text management software package STATUS to create the Wellington papers and Mountbatten papers databases. To access this database it is necessary for users

    (a) to be registered at Southampton as external users, with user identification and passwords recognized by the system;

    (b) to be familiar with the operating system of the university computer at Southampton, which forms the link with JANET; (some familiarity with local rules for computer use is also needed);

    (c) to be familiar with the query language of STATUS.

No cataloguing standard was needed, since the Wellington project is essentially not a set of descriptions so much as a published edition of texts. Standards for this type of work certainly do exist. They can be deduced from the experience of the historic publication projects familiar from 50 or 100 years ago, and are expressed in some very traditional-looking publications.[14]

Southampton University has joined with the Liddell-Hart Military Archives Centre, at King's College, London, to extend the range of the databases offered in this enterprise, using the same editorial technique, data structure and software.

By contrast, the approach of Glasgow University has been much more to abstract data from large groups of archival materials, and to produce databases which can be used in research or teaching by way of the statistical manipulation of primary data. To use the archival databases at Glasgow, users must be competent in the query language CAFS. Once this difficulty is overcome, online access to the material is easy, and files of data can be transferred to remote sites anywhere on the network. The archives department has collaborated in the development of software for the exploitation of these facilities, and in supporting the training of historians and other researchers in the techniques used. This approach to computing through historical research is typical of the European attitude to the exploitation of archives.

The Hartlib papers project at the University of Sheffield is also closely linked to historical research. It uses another text management software system, following what is becoming standard university practice.[15]

JANET will carry any form of electronic input, and several of these users are experimenting with document imaging.

Online databases which carry archival material exist or are planned in the Netherlands, Germany, France, Italy, Spain and Portugal. In all these cases the database is specific to archives, and not shared with libraries or bibliographic information. In France, the public videotex system Minitel is available to carry archival data, so that intending users can order documents in advance of their visit to a repository.

The Minitel experiment suggests a potential development which might be of great use to archivists. This is the concept of the local network. A prototype exists in Britain: this is the West Yorkshire Archives Service. WYAS is a service which has a central headquarters and six participating repositories in a region which has a common historical experience and urban character. The network is supported and controlled from headquarters, where a specialist archivist is based. Each repository has a terminal, in the form of a general-purpose PC linked through the telephone system. Authorities and standards are not strongly developed, but provide for a common format in which repositories report their accessions of new material.

The success of the WYAS network, which has an extremely small investment in staff and equipment, shows that local initiatives are likely to appear, and that they are likely to succeed in adding to standards of local service. Developing these into a national scheme must involve decision and investment centrally, however.

The development of a computer-based indexing system at the National Register of Archives, during 1988-90, is therefore of great potential significance. It is the only centrally-led development in archival data exchange since the end of the PROSPEC-SA experiment in 1977.

Since 1945 the NRA has acquired archive lists from some 1,300 repositories, and 3,000 private and institutional owners. Over 33,000 lists of substantial archive groups and collections are held, and some 60,000 lists of smaller and more miscellaneous accessions. Personal, subject and companies indexes are kept on all this, together with a central register of the basic details of title, location and NRA accession code for each list. Computerization of the indexes began in 1987, using a relational database system on a minicomputer. This involved recording all new information on the computer and making a retrospective conversion of the existing index entries (about 250,000 in all). New data continue to come in from all the various sources, in traditional form, and there is no plan to standardize this.[16]

Online access for the public began during 1989, and access to the personal names and subject indexes should be available by 1991-2, with limited public access. Full access will be possible when an extensive programme of checking and editing is finished, and there is an intention to set up a consultancy on networking the indexes, which might start work in 1992-3. The possibility of remote access and a national network must presumably attend the outcome of this.

An extension of the work of the NRA is the registration of archival surveys. The Royal Commission on Historical Manuscripts has published a list of these in progress in 1988, covering business, ecclesiastical, economic, genealogical, legal, literary and artistic, local, military, political, scientific and social topics.[17] The dozen or so noted as current at the time of publication are all recorded on personal computers, using commercial database software. The NRA's interest has probably brought about some degree of compatibility between the surveys, or at least mutual awareness, but each survey remains essentially a purpose-designed operation. Final outcomes include traditional publication of the findings, and the long-term use of the databases remains in doubt.

Document imaging

The National Archives of Spain has been the first to invest heavily in document imaging as a means of improving the relationship between lay users and the archives. The system has been developed first at the Archives of the Indies, at Seville, using the impetus provided by the fifth centenary celebrations of the discovery of America, in 1992.

In this system, an image of the original document is produced by digital scanning, and stored on an optical-digital disk. The quality of the reproduction is high, and with the use of high-resolution screens now commonly available with PCs, users can obtain a display which is actually easier to read than the original. Techniques now available allow the image to be cleaned, removing stains, extraneous marks, discoloration or writing appearing from the back. It is also possible to highlight and enlarge sectors of the image.

However, the image itself is not readable by the system, so that some other provision must be made to allow searching and retrieval. This is done by using a database which associates the image with a brief abstract of the document's contents. Much of the investment involved in setting up the system has gone in creating and inputting these descriptions.

It is intended in the first phase to transcribe in this way 10% of the holdings at Seville. This will produce a database of 9 million documents. Documents chosen for inclusion are those which are most in demand from users, so that it is expected that when complete the system will be used by up to 40% of readers.

A similar system is planned for the National Archives of Turkey.[18] The approach is particularly useful where the archive consists largely of materials which need specialist skills to read and interpret. In the Spanish example, most documents are in the handwriting of the 16th to 18th centuries; in the Turkish archives, the documents for inclusion will initially be those written in Ottoman script. Imaging is of course possible for material written in modern scripts, and here the discussion below on OCR techniques is relevant.

Future developments

The discussion of data exchange so far has been in historic terms. From this perspective, it would seem that future development is most likely in the spread of large shared bibliographic databases, and the standards and authorities that go with them. However, a glance round the world of information technology might suggest that some development will go in other directions. In this section, some of the alternatives will be considered.[19]

Optical character recognition (OCR)

Software and hardware are now becoming available which will allow large quantities of unstructured text to be entered into electronic textbases, and which will allow this material to be searched rapidly by relatively inexpert users.

The main use for these developments so far has been in the creation of literary databases (*textbases*). Most developed countries now have very large literary textbases, covering whole sectors of their national literature. Other projects are based upon the work of a particular author (such as Shakespeare or St Paul), or a particular body of published literature (such as the *Patrologia Latina*), or on biblical or historical texts. Promoters of the technology expect that there will be wide new applications for it, not only in publishing and textual criticism, but wherever data has to be stored and used.

As a large body of textual information which is part of the common heritage, the archives of a culture may be compared with its literature. It is only a matter of time before there is a recognition that they should be available through electronic tools.

Archival descriptions are not unstructured text, but there is often a backlog accumulation of them which does not conform to modern standards, or to any standard at all. If computer systems arrive which can easily store large amounts of text without first demanding that it be restructured, and which provide very rapid means of retrieving information, then much of the tedious work of data preparation or subsequent conversion could be avoided.

As far as the technical translation of written data into electronic files is concerned, systems now exist which can carry this out cheaply.

Optical character recognition (OCR) systems have existed for some time, but in the past they have either depended on reading special fonts in the input material, or have been very expensive. Large organizations have long used forms of OCR to read data from standard forms (for example, a tick written into a box).

OCR systems using techniques of digitizing patterns on a paper have been developed which can read handwriting, and even solve palaeographical problems. Such a system is used by the Genealogical Society of Salt Lake City. They have been too expensive for use by most repositories. Also, if the system is regarded as an alternative to other methods of treatment, the input process has been just below the level of economic effectiveness. Levels of accuracy in these systems are quite high – over 95% commonly – but still require that there should be a human monitor.

Cheap OCR scanners which are capable of reading ordinary typescript at similar levels of accuracy are now available, and have been tested at the National Archives of the USA. Scanners are also used as input methodology in the Spanish imaging project. As far as typescript text is concerned, the possible usefulness of this hardware is greatly increased by software packages which help to give the input data a usable structure, by writing in tags which serve to identify fields.

SGML

The use of such tags would be much more universal if there were more appreciation by archivists of the value of the Standard Generalized Mark-up Language (SGML). This standard sets a value for a series of tags, which can be written into a text in order to establish the structural elements it contains. These may include an hierarchy of titles and subtitles, main and subordinate sections, and formatting instructions. It would be desirable for SGML tags to be assigned to MAD2 models of description. Compatible tags have been used by the British Library Department of Manuscripts in setting out manuscript catalogue entries for publication.

Natural-language searching

Reference was made in Chapter 5 to the development of natural-language searching of databases. This technology is advancing fast with the arrival of very fast modern computers, such as those with parallel processing. It is not expected that it will be available for ordinary users for some years yet.[20]

Up to now, systems which aim at presenting material for online search by non-specialized users have not commended themselves to archivists. They demand not only that the users should be trained in the techniques of searching, but also that there should be sufficient in the way of authority control to make the database manageable. Searching techniques have not up to now been taught in archival training schools, and the authority files do not yet exist. If searching by external users is visualized, the problems become vastly greater.

Natural-language searching might possibly offer an alleviation of this problem. These are systems in which a series of search questions may be put to the computer in direct speech, without the need for them to be translated into a controlled format.

For example, in SQL, which is a common online search language, a request must be formulated like this:

Select title, date, location –	\<field names\>
from descriptionfile –	\<filename\>
where title like '%EC%' –	\<search terms\>
order by title	arrangement of output

Any small variation in the order, wording or punctuation of this request will result in an error report.

In natural-language searching, this request could be input like this:

What is the title, date and whereabouts of any record referring to the EC? Give an alphabetical listing.

Much more complex questions can be formulated, using all the usual operators. Questions like 'what is the total population of countries where the ratio of doctors to population is greater than 10,000 and where the rate of population increase is greater than 4.1%?' would be possible where a suitable data file existed.

One supposes that this much more unrestricted method of questioning will greatly reduce the difficulty which many users feel when trying to search a computer database. The system internally translates the question or series of questions into an SQL-like sequence and then carries out the search. However, it is important to realize that this is the limit of the system's power: when this operation has been done, the effectiveness of the natural-language search is the same as that of the technically formulated-language search. The system can only look for specified keywords (albeit perhaps linked to a set of other terms in a thesaurus) in a specified file. If it does not find the keyword, it reports negatively. A negative reply from an online search may be more misleading than a failed scan of hard-copy finding aids.

Alternative media

The success of online databases (and their wide and continuing spread over the world) has possibly drawn some attention away from the development of alternative forms of information storage which are becoming common. These media offer the possibility that offline data exchange may be more practical for archives than online.

The most immediately practical of these new media is probably the compact disk with read-only memory (CD-ROM). Initially developed as an alternative to the now traditional plastic disk for recording music, the CD-ROM is now a normal part of the tools available to reference libraries. Today, many reference books are published in this form, which offers advantages over previously available formats, such as microfilm. It is easy for publishers to update the information, since they can write it anew to fresh disks; postage costs are minimal, and very large amounts of text can be entered on a small space (in fact, this last factor is a problem, since only very large databases are truly economic). As a form of publication, the CD-ROM is well established.

Since archival descriptions are published material, they should be apt for inclusion. The attractiveness of the CD-ROM for this is increased by the fact that since each disk is a separate publication, there is less need for elaborate authority controls or cataloguing standards (although there is need for some, especially where it is finding aids, rather than full text or calendars, which is being entered). Searching techniques are of course needed for access, but can be helped by including indexes and chapter headings, etc.

The optical-digital disk is a further extension of this medium. These disks are as yet too expensive to be widely available for most repositories, and there is as yet no general format standard. They are in use in the largest institutions. The Public Record Office intends to use them as part of its records management programme for machine-readable records. The Library of Congress uses them for the storage and cataloguing of its collection of prints and watercolours.

There are many other applications actively in use throughout the world.

These disks are generically termed WORM (Write Once, Read Many times) disks. They are multi-media, and varieties of them can be used to store newly composed text, facsimiles of original documents, pictorial or graphic material, sound or moving pictures, or a combination of these. Control information can be written in, so that interactive disks are possible. With these, the user can type instructions which have the effect of moving straight to related parts of the database, putting search questions and so on. Since the disks are of durable material, no special storage conditions are needed in which to keep them.

As a means of publishing archival texts, including finding aids, this medium has considerable appeal. As the technology becomes cheaper and more common, this appeal will develop strongly. It has the great advantage over CD-ROM that texts can be visually displayed. Users can therefore scan lists of contents and indexes and get the same direct visual understanding of the document which they would get from handling the original typescript; or they can scan facsimiles of original documents. The need for descriptive standards and for fully worked-out authority controls is minimized.

Hypermedia

With the advent of very rapid computing, the development of the various forms of hypermedia is likely to be of interest, at least to the users of archival materials. The concept behind this development is that keywords (or symbols) which exist in one electronic text, can be linked to other cognate words or symbols in other texts, or in other media. When these links are established, users can switch from one access point to any or all of the others, crossing any boundaries of medium on the way. The result would be like following a train of thought, and it would be possible to draw together a mass of knowledge on a theme chosen by the user.

Limited versions of this hyperlinkage do exist, and have achieved a certain amount of success as teaching aids. Some scepticism may perhaps be expressed about the prospects for its success on a larger scale. Clearly the technology is capable of establishing the links between media. What is in doubt is the ability of human operators, within the ordinary constraints of academic life, to carry out the necessary linguistic analysis. Once again, practical systems are not likely to be available before the end of the century.

The archive services of the future

It may be agreed that the body of principles which has informed the work of archivists in the last two centuries (part of which has been the subject of this book) is in the process of being radically modified by the appearance of quite new forms of record. New principles of operation are beginning to appear so that the administration of the new archives can proceed. The new forms of record and archive are making their appearance in many repositories which are otherwise quite traditional, as well as in specialized repositories.

Nevertheless, the traditional archives remain, and in many parts of the world traditionally based records are still being produced in great numbers. For many administrations, the new methods of communication have not yet arrived: in some parts of the world they may never arrive. A certain degree of deliberate conservatism is therefore suitable.

What we have to do now is to devise ways in which the archives and records services which are based on traditional documentary forms should benefit from the advances made in information management. These advances should do something to overcome the biggest single difficulty in making archives useful: the backlog of material which is not fully controlled and retrievable. The effort of the present should be towards bringing traditional archive holdings up to the standard of the best contemporary information service. If that could really be done, we would have experienced a revolution in our use of an important information medium.

Notes and references

1 Historical Manuscripts Commission, London.
2 Walne, P., 'The record commissions, 1800-1837', in Ranger, F. (ed.), *Prisca munimenta: studies in archival and administrative history, presented to Dr A.E.J. Hollaender*, University of London Press, 1973, 9-18.
3 Jenkinson, C. H., *A manual of archive administration*, 2nd edn (revised), Lund Humphries, 1965, Part II, section 8, 'The secondary duties of the archivist', 125-32.

4 Ellis, R.H., 'The Historical Manuscripts Commission, 1869-1969', *Journal of the Society of Archivists*, 3, 1969, 441.

5 Hudson, J.P., *Manuscripts indexing*, British Library, Department of Manuscripts, 1979.

6 Galbraith, V.H., 'The approach to research', in *An introduction to the use of the Public Records*, Oxford, 1934, 66-88.

7 *NIDS UK & Ireland*, Chadwyck-Healey Ltd, Cambridge.

8 All standards are summarized in *Archival description standards: establishing a process for their development and implementation*, Report of the Working Group on Standards for Archival Description, Feb. 1990, Appendix I, 65-78.

9 The difference between 6xx and 7xx entries is a matter of debate among users: Weber, L.B., 'Record formatting: MARC AMC', in Smiralgia, R.P. (ed.), *Describing archival materials: the use of the MARC AMC format*, Haworth Press, New York and London, 1990, 117-43.

10 The possibility of developing a UKMARC AMC version was examined by the Archival Description Project at Liverpool University in 1988-9, and is under discussion by the British Library Bibliographic Services and user groups in 1992.

11 For example, by the Tate Gallery Archives. Information from A. Hopkinson, Systems Development Officer.

12 Information from Dr Jan Dahlin, Provincial Archivist of Lund. Evans, M. J. and Weber, L. B. (eds.), *MARC for archives and manuscripts: a compendium of practice*, Society of American Archivists, Chicago, 1985.

13 Joint Academic Network. See below in this chapter, p.172-3.

14 For example, British Records Association, *Notes for the guidance of editors of record publications*, London, 1946.

15 At the time of writing, but possibly not later, the software system was BRS/Search, which, following an evaluation, had been adopted as the preferred text-retrieval system for British universities: Bain, M. *et al.*, *Free text retrieval systems: a review and evaluation*, Taylor Graham, London, 1989.

16 Information derived from the report of the working party on archival data exchange, to the National Council on Archives, 1990.

17 Royal Commission on Historical Manuscripts, *Surveys of historical manuscripts in the United Kingdom: a select bibliography*, London, HMSO, 1989.

18 Information from Dr Ismet Binark, Director of the Archives of the Republic of Turkey, Ankara, 1991.
19 All published information on computing is obsolete as soon as it appears. This section draws largely on Weir, T.E., 'New automation techniques for archivists', in Bradsher, J.G. ed.), *Managing archives and archival institutions*, Mansell, London, 1988, 134-47. By dealing mainly with the underlying principles, this chapter achieved some degree of longevity.
20 British Library, *Information 2000*, London, 1991.

Suggestions for reading and reference

Today there are many thousands of books and articles on subjects connected with archivology. Some of them are of continuing value, but (like similar publications in other fields) some are only interesting as landmarks on the road of progress; many are obsolescent or dead. There are excellent means of reference in all the developed countries, and in developing countries there are organizations that work to disseminate information and pass on reference materials. It would make little sense to produce a lengthy bibliography in a single book, much of which would rapidly lose currency.

The list of materials which appears below is restricted to those which seem to be of current value for reference and to support training, together with a chosen few which for the moment are important in shaping future development. The needs of first-entry student archivists have been kept primarily in mind.

Selection has also been confined to the subjects with which this book has been most concerned: description and the development of standards for the use of archival materials; automation insofar as it has affected this; and training. An effort has been made to exclude materials which are not quite recent.

The main means of access to current journal articles in the central aspects of archivology, is *Library and information science abstracts* (LISA), published monthly, and also available as a CD-ROM. The principal journals in the English language are: the *Journal of the Society of Archivists*; *Archives*; *Business archives* (UK); *The American archivist* (USA); *Archivaria* (Canada); *Archives and manuscripts* (Australia); *Archifacts* (New Zealand). International sources are now impossible to ignore. The ICA has launched a new journal, *Janus*, which has some important material in it and may prove itself. The General Information Programme of Unesco's RAMP series now contains several essential manuals of practice, and is continuing. The former Unesco journal covering these subjects has been replaced by *Information development*.

General bibliographies

Duchein, M. (comp.), *Basic international bibliography of archive administration. Archivum XXV,*. K.G. Saur, *1978.*

Evans, F.B. (comp.), *The history of archives administration: a select bibliography,* Unesco, Documentation Libraries and Archives, Bibliographies and reference works 6, Paris, 1979.

General archivology

Abraham, Terry, 'Collection policy or documentation strategy: theory and practice', *The American archivist,* **54**, 1991, 44-52.

Bowden, R, *Guidelines for the management of professional associations in the fields of archives, library and information work,* Unesco, Paris, 1989.

Bradsher, J.G. (ed.), *Managing archives and archival institutions,* Mansell, London, 1988.

Cook, M., *The management of information from archives,* Gower, Aldershot, 1986.

Couture, C. and Rousseau, J.Y., *Les archives aux XXe siècle: une réponse aux besoins de l'administration et de la recherche,* Université de Montreal, 1982.

Daniels, M.F. and Walch, T. (eds), *A modern archives reader: basic readings on archival theory and practice,* National Archives and Records Service, Washington, DC, 1984.

Delmas, B. *et al.* (eds), *Vocabulaire des archives,* Archivistique et diplomatique contemporaines, Les dossiers de la normalisation, AFNOR, Paris, 1986.

Dunhill, Rosemary, 'The National Council on Archives: its role in professional thinking and development', *Journal of the Society of Archivists,* **11**, 1990, 32-6.

Evans, F.B. *et al.* (comps), 'A basic glossary for archivists, manuscript curators and records managers', *The American archivist,* **37**, 1974, 415-33.

Foster, Janet and Sheppard, Julia, *British archives: a guide to archival sources in the U.K.,* 2nd edn, Macmillan, 1989.

Healy, Susan, 'The classification of modern government records in England and Australia', *Journal of the Society of Archivists,* **11**, 1990, 17-20.

Heredia Herrera, A., *Archivistica general, teoria y practica,* Servicio de Publicaciones de la Diputacion de Sevilla, 1986.

International Council on Archives, *Dictionary of archival terminology*, Evans, F.B., Himley, F.J. and Walne, P. (comps), ICA Handbooks Vol. 3, K.G. Saur, Munich, 1984.

Jenkinson, C.H., *A manual of archive administration*, original version 1922; 2nd edn (revised), Lund Humphries, London, 1965.

Ketelaar, E., *Archival and records management legislation and regulations*, Unesco, Paris, 1985.

Knightbridge, A.A.H., *Archive legislation in the United Kingdom*, Society of Archivists, 1985.

Lodolini, Elio, *Archivistica: principi e problemi*, Franco Angeli, Milano, 1984.

Mazikana, Peter C., *Archives and records management for decision makers: a RAMP study*, Unesco, Paris, 1990.

Methven, Patricia J., 'Performance measurement and standards', *Journal of the Society of Archivists*, **11**, 1990, 78-84.

Pederson, A. (ed.), *Keeping archives*, Australian Society of Archivists, Sydney, 1987.

Raspin, G.E.A., *The transfer of private papers to repositories*, Society of Archivists information leaflet, 1988.

Rhoads, J.B., *The applicability of UNISIST guidelines and ISO international standards to archive administration and records management: a RAMP study*, Unesco, Paris, 1982.

Rhoads, J.B., *The role of archives and records management in national information systems: a RAMP study*, Unesco, Paris, 1983; revised edn, 1989.

Roper, Michael, *Directory of national standards relating to archives administration and records management*, Unesco, Paris, 1986.

Roper, Michael. 'Unesco's records and archives management programme (RAMP)', *Journal of the Society of Archivists*, **12** 1991, 63-5.

Royal Commission on Historical Manuscripts, *Surveys of historical manuscripts in the United Kingdom: a select bibliography*, HMSO, London, 1989.

Schellenberg, T.R., *Modern archives, principles and techniques*, University of Chicago Press, 1956.

Schellenberg, T.R., *The management of archives*, Columbia University Press, 1965.

Scott, P.J., 'Archives and administrative change: some methods and approaches', *Archives and manuscripts*, **9**, 1981, 3-18.

Seton, R.E., *The preservation and administration of private archives*, Unesco, Paris, 1984.

Smith, B.S., '"British Archives" and acquisitions policies', *Journal of the Society of Archivists*, **11**, 1990, 47-51.

Smith, B.S., 'A standard for record repositories', *Journal of the Society of Archivists*, **12**, 1990, 114-22.

Thomas, D.L., *Study on control of security and storage of holdings*, Unesco, Paris, 1986.

Turton, A. (ed.), *Managing business archives*, Butterworth-Heinemann in association with the Business Archives Council, 1991.

Vaughan, A., *International reader in the management of library, information and archives services*, Unesco, Paris, 1987.

Walne, P. and Mabbs, A.W. (eds), *Modern archives administration and records management: a RAMP reader*, Unesco, Paris, 1985.

Archival automation and its effects

Arnold, B. and Rowell, H., 'The Australian Archives records information system (RINSE)', *Archives and manuscripts*, **17**, 1989.

Bain, M., *et al.*, *Free text retrieval systems: a review and evaluation*, Taylor Graham, London, 1989.

Campbell, T.M., 'Archives and information management', *Archivaria*, **28**, 1989.

Casey, Michael, 'The electronic information industry in Europe', *Journal of librarianship and information science*, **23**, 1991, 21-36.

Dempsey, Lorcan (ed.), *Bibliographic access in Europe: first international conference*, Proceedings of a conference organized by the Centre for Bibliographic Management, University of Bath, Gower, Aldershot, 1990.

Dollar, Charles, *Electronic records management and archives in international organisations: a RAMP study with guidelines*, Unesco, Paris, 1986. Also *The impact of information technologies on archival principles and practices: some considerations*, circulated by the author in successive versions from 1990.

Fahmy, E. and Barnard, D.T., 'Adding hypertext links to an archive of documents', *Canadian journal of information science*, **15**, 1990, 25-41.

Foster, C.D., 'Online database searching: the literature of archives and

187

manuscripts administration', *Proceedings of an international conference on databases in the humanities and social sciences, Auburn University*, ed. McCrank, L.J., Learned Information Ltd, Medford, New Jersey, 1989.

Gavrel, K., *Conceptual problems posed by electronic records: a RAMP study*, Unesco, Paris, 1990.

Green, Adam, *The development of policies and plans in archival automation: a RAMP study with guidelines*, Unesco, Paris, 1991.

Kitching, Christopher, *The impact of computerisation on finding aids: a RAMP study*, Unesco, Paris, 1991.

Michelson, Avra, *Expert systems technology and its implication for archives*, National Archives and Records Administration, Technical Information Paper 9, Washington, DC, 1991.

Pepler, Jonathan, 'The impact of computers on classification theory', *Journal of the Society of Archivists*, **11**, 1990, 27-31.

Roe, Kathleen D., 'The automation odyssey: library and archives system design considerations', *Cataloging and classification quarterly*, **11**, 1990, 145-62.

Walford, J., Gillett, H. and Post, J.B. 'Introducing computers to the record office: theory and practice', *Journal of the Society of Archivists*, **9**, 1988, 21-9.

Williams, C.J., 'Computerisation in the Clwyd Record Office', *Journal of the Society of Archivists*, **10**, 1989, 66-74.

Woolgar, C.M., 'Marshalling the data: large collections of personal papers and the cataloguer', *Proceedings of the annual conference*, Business Archives Council, 1990.

Archival description, standards, and data exchange

Bearman, David, 'Description standards: a framework', *The American archivist*, **52**, 1989, 514-19.

Black, Elizabeth, *Authority control: a manual for archivists*, Bureau of Canadian Archivists, Planning Committee on Descriptive Standards, Ottawa, 1991.

Broom, A., 'Standards for archives: the work of the British Standards Institution related to archives', *Journal of the Society of Archivists*, **8**, 1987, 174-80.

Bureau of Canadian Archivists, *Toward descriptive standards: a report and recommendations of the Canadian working group on archival descriptive standards*, Ottawa, 1985.

Cook, M. and Procter, M., *Manual of archival description*, 2nd edn (MAD2), Gower, 1990.

Evans, M.J. and Weber, L.B., *MARC for archives and manuscripts: a compendium of practice*, Society of American Archivists, Chicago, 1985.

Fox, Michael J., 'Descriptive cataloging for archival materials', *Cataloging and classification quarterly*, 11, 1990, 17-34.

Gilliland, A., 'Automating intellectual access to archives', *Library trends*, 1988, 495-623.

Gonzalez, Pedro, 'Las nuevas tecnologias y la descripcion de archivos', *IRARGI, Revista de Archivistica*, 4, 1991, 135-66.

Gracy, D.B. II, *Archives and manuscripts: arrangement and description*, Basic Manuals Series, Society of American Archivists, Chicago, 1989.

Gredley, E. and Hopkinson, A., *Exchanging bibliographic data: MARC and other international formats*, Library Association, London, 1990.

Hensen, S.L., *Archives, personal papers and manuscripts: a cataloging manual for archival repositories, historical societies and manuscripts libraries*, 2nd edn, Society of American Archivists, Chicago, 1989.

Hickerson, H.T., 'Archival information exchange and the role of bibliographic networks', *Library trends*, 36, 1988.

Hildesheimer, F., *Guidelines for preparation of general guides to national archives: a RAMP study*, Unesco, Paris, 1983.

International Council on Archives, Ad Hoc Commission on Archival Description, *Statement of principles regarding archival description* (revised). Also *ISAD(G): Standard general archival description*, National Archives of Canada, 1992.

International Federation of Library Associations and Institutions (IFLA), *International standard bibliographical descriptions*, IFLA, London, from 1977.

Jones, David R., 'Archival cataloguing: a select bibliography', *Business archives, principles and practice*, 61, 1991, 55-9.

Michelson, Avra, 'Description and reference in the age of automation', *The American archivist*, 50, 1987, 192-208.

Miller, F.M., *Arranging and describing archives and manuscripts*, Archives Fundamentals Series, Society of American Archivists, Chicago, 1990.

Sahli, N., *MARC for archives and manuscripts: the AMC format*, Society of American Archivists, Chicago, 1985.

Smiraglia, Richard P. (ed.), *Describing archival materials: the use of the MARC AMC format*, Haworth Press, New York & London, 1990.

Society of American Archivists, *Archival description standards: establishing a process for their development and implementation*, Report of the working group on standards for archival description, Feb. 1990.

Taylor, H.A., *The arrangement and description of archival materials*, ICA Handbooks Vol. 2, K.G. Saur, Munich, 1980.

Records management

Cameron, Alan, 'Records management and conservation: conflicting objectives', *Journal of the Society of Archivists*, **12**, 1991, 36-41.

Charman, D., *Records surveys and schedules*, Unesco, Paris, 1984.

Doyle, M. and Frenière, A., *La préparation de manuels de gestion de documents a l'intention des administrations publiques: une étude RAMP*, Unesco, Paris, 1991.

Emmerson, P., *Records retention*, Business Archives Council, Record Aids No. 3, 1983.

Emmerson, P., *How to manage your records*, ICSA, Cambridge, 1989.

Hampson, Jill, 'Filing practice: an annotated bibliography', *Business archives: principles and practice*, **59**, 1990, 69-74.

Holloway, S., *Methodology handbook for information managers*, Gower, Aldershot, 1989.

James, S., *Records management: an introduction*, TFPL, London, 1989.

McCarthy, Gavan, 'Records disposal in the modern environment', *Archives and manuscripts*, **18**, 1990, 39-51.

Mander, D., 'Records management in London local authorities', *Journal of the Society of Archivists*, **10**, 1989, 14-19.

Morddel, A., 'Records management education in Britain: groping in the dusk', *Records management quarterly*, **23**, 1989, 3-11.

National Archives of Canada, *Management of government records: guidelines on computer-assisted records management*, Ottawa, 1988.

Orbell, John, 'The introduction of a computer-based modern records control system at Barings merchant bank', *Business archives*, **55**, 1988, 29-38.

Penn, I.A., Morddel, A., Pennix, G. and Smith, K., *Records management handbook*, Gower, Aldershot, 1989.

Williams, R.V., 'Records management education: an IRM perspective', *Records management quarterly*, **21**, 1987, 36-40.

Professional training

Association des Archivistes de Quebec, 'Bibliographie sur la formation professionnelle', *Archives, revue de l'Association*, **20**, 1989, 77-82.

Association of Canadian Archivists, 'Guidelines for MAS programs (Masters in Archival Studies)', *Archivaria*, **31**, 1989, 60-89.

Bowden, R., 'Harmonisation of education and training programmes for library, information and archival personnel', *Education for information*, **5**, 1987, 207-33.

Carucci, Paola, 'L'adaptation des programmes de formation aux developpements modernes dans le domaine de l'archivistique', *Janus*, **1**, 1990, 44-7.

Clubb, Clare, 'Training for business archivists in the United Kingdom', *Business archives*, **61**, 1991, 1-12.

Cook, M., *Guidelines for curriculum development in records management and the administration of modern archives: a RAMP study*, Unesco, Paris, 1982.

Cook, M., *Guidelines on curriculum development in information technology for librarians, documentalists and archivists*, Unesco, Paris, 1986.

Cooper, M.L. and Lois, F., 'Education and training of the information professional', *Annual review of information science and technology*, **24**, 1989, 295-341.

Correa, A.F., *Equivalence des qualifications et reciprocité*, IFLA Publications 50, 1989, 309-42.

Cox, R.J., 'Textbooks, archival education and the archival profession', *Public historian*, **12**, 1990, 73-81.

Delmas, Bruno (ed.), *Actes du premier colloque international sur la formation des archivistes*, International Council on Archives, Paris, 1988.

Dunhill, R. and Short, C., 'The training of archivists 1970-1990: an overview', *Journal of the Society of Archivists*, **12**, 1991, 42-50.

191

Fishbein, M., *A model curriculum for the education and training of archivists in automation*, Unesco, Paris, 1985.

Fontein, F. and Bernhard, P., *Guidelines for writing objectives in librarianship, information science and archives administration*, Unesco, Paris, 1988.

Franz, Eckhard, 'Curriculum content for various levels of archival training', *Janus*, **1**, 1990, 27-33.

Harrison, Helen P., 'Training for audiovisual archivists', *Audio-visual librarian*, **16**, 1990, 116-22.

International Council on Archives, *La formation professionnelle des archivistes. Archivum*, **34**, K.G. Saur, Munich etc., 1988.

Lodolini, Elio, 'La formacion profesional y las escuelas de archivistica', in *De archivos y archivistas: homenaje a Aurelio Tanodi*, Organization of American States, Washington, DC, 1987.

Marcoux, Y. (ed.), *Standards and guidelines applied to archival institutions, archival education programs and ethics*, CCIDA Bibliographies 50, National Archives Library, Ottawa, 1990.

Menne-Haritz, A., *Ueberlieferung gestalten. Der Archivschule Marburg zum 40 Jahrestag ihrer Grundung*, Archivschule Marburg, 1989.

'Adaptation of existing training programmes to modern developments in the archival field', *Janus*, **1**, 1990, 38-43.

Sigmond, J.P., 'The role of associations of archivists in continuing training', *Proceedings of X International Congress on Archives*, Bonn, 1984.

Society of American Archivists, *Guidelines for the development of post-appointment and continuing education and training programs*, SAA, Chicago, Dec. 1990.

Society of Archivists, Diploma in archives administration: course notes, 1980.

Society of Archivists, Archives assistants' training pack, 1986.

Thurston, A., 'New directions in archival training', *Janus*, **1**, 1990, 48-52.

Unesco, General Information Programme and UNISIST, *Curriculum development for the training of personnel in moving image and recorded sound archives*, Paris, 1990.

Wimalaratne, K.D.G., 'Training in archives and records management for third-world countries, its impact on development', *Janus*, **1**, 1990, 7-12.

Appraisal

Cox, R.J. and Samuels, H.W., 'The archivist's first responsibility: a research agenda to improve the identification and retention of records of enduring value', *The American archivist*, **51**, 1988, 1-2.

Guptil, Marilla, *Archival appraisal of records of international organisations: a RAMP study with guidelines*, Unesco, Paris, 1985.

Haas, J.K., Samuels, H.W. and Simmons, B.T., *Appraising the records of science and technology: a guide*, Massachusetts Institute of Technology, 1985.

Harrison, Helen P. and Schuurma, R.L., *The archival appraisal of sound recordings and related materials*, Unesco, Paris, 1987.

Hull, F., *The use of sampling techniques in the retention of records: a RAMP study*, Unesco, Paris, 1981.

Kula, S., *The archival appraisal of moving images: a RAMP study with guidelines*, Unesco, Paris, 1983.

Leary, W.H., *The archival appraisal of photographs*, Unesco, Paris, 1985.

Naugler, Harold, *The archival appraisal of machine-readable records*, Unesco, Paris, 1984.

Peace, N.E. (ed.), *Archival choices: managing the historical record in an age of abundance*, Lexington Books, 1984.

Rene-Bazin, Paule, 'La création et la collecte des nouvelles archives', *Rassegna degli archivi di stato*, **48**, 1988, 14-50.

Richmond, Lesley, 'A national documentation strategy for business', *Business archives*, **59**, 1990, 37-46.

User services

Duchein, M., *Obstacles to the access, use and transfer of information from archives: a RAMP study*, Unesco, Paris, 1983.

Holbert, S.E., *Archives and manuscripts: reference and access*, Basic Manuals Series, Society of American Archivists, Chicago, 1977.

Mchombu, K.J., 'User studies: how to identify potential and actual user needs', in Johnson, I.M. *et al.* (eds), *Harmonisation of education and training programmes*, IFLA Publications 49, K.G. Saur, Munich etc., 1989, 150-64.

Taylor, H.A., *Archival services and the concept of the user*, Unesco, Paris, 1984.

Whalen, L. (ed.), *Reference services in archives*, Haworth Press, 1986.

Yates, N., 'Marketing the record office: new directions in archival public relations', *Journal of the Society of Archivists*, 9, 1988, 69–75.

Index

198

199

international description standard
see ISAD(G)
International Federation of
Documentalists 162
International Federation of Library
Associations 162
International Standard
Bibliographic Description *see*
ISBD
International standards 51, 163
International Standards
Organisation 162
Internet 169, 172
interpretative sciences 29
inversion 132-3
inverted files 138, 148, 151
ISAD(G) 102-3, 129-30
ISBD 162, 165-6
issue of records 41-5, 48-9
item descriptions 38, 94-6, 98,
121-2
  in reading room 119
  models for 107, 115, 117
  physical data in 107
  secondary 97
item level 40, 67
  conventional 79
  criteria for determining 73
  defined 68-9
  title 82

JANET 57, 169, 172-3
Jenkinson, Sir Hilary 6, 9, 64, 67-8,
72, 91, 158
Joint Academic Network, *see* JANET

keywords 137-8, 141, 148
  in search 179
  in AACR2 166
  rule of 129
  strings 108
  subfields 139
King's College 173
KWIC 140-1
KWOC 140-1

language of materials 64, 102
late returns 44

latest order
  rule of 64
left column 120
legal services 50
legal usage 4, 6
legal values 31-2, 34, 50
legibility of image 175
legislation 19, 25
Leicestershire Record Office 147
leisure services 17
length of descriptions 97
letters
  see correspondence
levels of arrangement 39, 64, 73,
94, 96-7
  absent 69, 73, 77-8, 80
  criteria for 69
  criteria for setting 72
  defined 67-8
  fundamental 69, 76
  hierarchy of 67
  models for 108
  numbers 40, 68, 106, 120-1
  defined 67
levels of classification 71
levels of description 97, 102,
161-2, 166
  data elements for 107
  defined 93
  determine models 103
  displaying 120-1
  in databases 167
  models for 107, 109
  reflected in reference codes 84
  standard 79·
libraries
  in organizations 14, 16, 28
  public 17, 19
library
  catalogues 141, 170, 172
  network 146
Library of Congress 164-5, 179
  Subject Headings 143, 172
Liddell-Hart Military Archives 173
life cycle of records 29, 31
linguistic analysis 181
linkages
  between levels 115, 119, 165

202

204